Dear Customer,

Thank you for your purchase.
I hope you enjoy your time with this book.
I invite you to explore my full range of products on Amazon.
I create original books, including coloring and activity books for children,
teenagers, and adults, available in multiple languages.
Please check back from time to time to stay updated on the latest news.
You can also visit the author's Amazon website using the provided QR
code.

BIG HUGS
Eva Rose

CA

MX

US

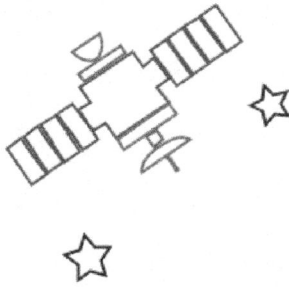

THIS BOOK BELONG TO:

OBSERVATION LOG

DATE:			TIME:	
OBSERVER:				
LOCATION:				
SEEING:	① ② ③ ④ ⑤	TRANSPARENCY:	① ② ③ ④ ⑤	

OBJECTS I SAW

○ MOON   ○ STAR   ○ PLANET   ○ COMET

○ CONSTELLATION   ○ GALAXY   ○ _____

FIELD DRAWING

Lunar+Solar Eclipses 2024

ECLIPSE DATE	LUNAR/SOLAR	WHERE IT'S VISIBLE IN THE WORLD
MARCH 24-25	PENUMBRAL LUNAR ECLIPSE	SOUTHEAST EUROPE, EAST ASIA, AUSTRALIA, NORTH AMERICA, SOUTH AMERICA, PACIFIC
APRIL 8	TOTAL SOLAR ECLIPSE	WEST EUROPE, AUSTRALIA, NORTH AMERICA, SOUTH AMERICA, PACIFIC
SEPT 17-18	PARTIAL LUNAR ECLIPSE	EUROPE, SW ASIA, AFRICA, NORTH AMERICA, SOUTH AMERICA, INDIA
OCT 2	ANNULAR SOLAR ECLIPSE	SOUTH AMERICA + ANTARCTICA
OCT 17	ANNULAR SOLAR ECLIPSE	ASIA, AUSTRALIA, NORTH AMERICA

Monday, April 8 th, 2024
Times and Places - US

start - 06:27 HST
end - 16:41 EDT
duration - 1h, 7m, 58s

Cleveland, OH
3:13 PM EDT
3 min 49 sec

Indianapolis, IN
3:06 PM EDT
3 min 49 sec

Burlington, VT
3:26 PM EDT
3 min 15 sec

Toledo, OH
3:12 PM EDT
1 min 53 sec

San Antonio, TX
1:33 PM CDT
2 min 03 sec

Austin, TX
1:36 PM CDT
1 min 44 sec

Buffalo, NY
3:18 PM EDT
3 min 45 sec

Little Rock, AR
1:51 PM CDT
2 min 20 sec

Erie, PA
3:16 PM EDT
3 min 40 sec

Dallas, TX
1:40 PM CDT
3 min 51 sec

Monday, April 8 th, 2024
Times and Places - Canada

start - 10:40 PDT
end - 18:18 NDT
duration - 34m, 4s

Partial Starting
10:40 PDT
near
Swordfish Island

Totality Starting
15:12 EDT
near
Ballast Island

Totality Ending
17:16 NDT
near
North Head

Partial Ending
18:18 NDT
near
West Landing

Monday, April 8 th, 2024
Times and Places - Mexico

start - 09:32 PDT
end - 14:56 EST
duration - 40m, 43s

Partial Starting
09:32 PDT
near
Punta Rocosa

Totality Starting
10:51 MST
near
Monte Medina

Totality Ending
12:32 CST
near
Jiménez

Partial Ending
14:56 EST
near
Boca Nueva

Types of Solar Eclipses

PARTIAL

ANNULAR

TOTAL

How It Works

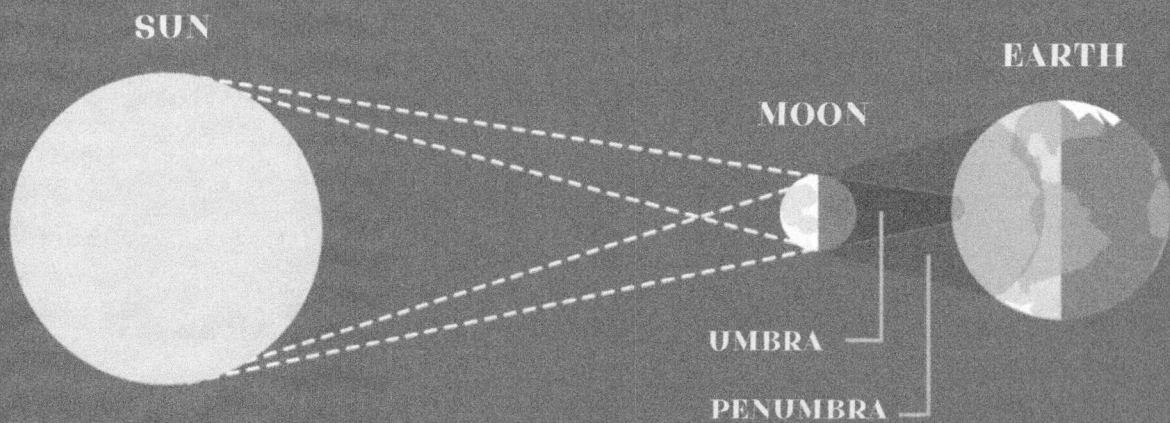

SUN

MOON

EARTH

UMBRA

PENUMBRA

What is a Solar Eclipse?

An eclipse is a moment when the Moon covers the Sun for a while.

It's like playing hide and seek, but in space!

There are three main types of solar eclipses:

Total eclipse: This is when the Moon almost completely covers the Sun. It looks like the Moon is just blocking the Sun, and we on Earth see it getting dark during the day. It's a really cool phenomenon!

Partial eclipse: This is when the Moon partially covers the Sun. It means it's not completely covered, but it looks like a piece of it is hidden, so it's not as bright as usual.

Annular eclipse: This one is a bit different. When the Moon is farther from Earth, it might look smaller in the sky and won't completely cover the Sun. As a result, when it covers the Sun, there will be a ring of light around it because it won't cover it entirely.

It's like we're playing hide and seek - sometimes the Moon completely covers the Sun, and sometimes only a piece of it. But every time, it's an incredible cosmic show!

How to Stay Safe?

Eyes looking directly at the Sun during a regular day can get damaged, and when an eclipse occurs, the Sun becomes even brighter and more hazardous to the eyes.

Here are a few ways to safely view an eclipse:

Solar eclipse glasses: Wear special solar eclipse glasses designed for observing the eclipse. These glasses protect your eyes from harmful sunlight.

Eclipse filters: You can also use special filters or telescopes equipped with eclipse filters. They also protect your eyes.

Image projection: You can create a simple way to watch the eclipse without looking directly at the Sun. Take a piece of paper, cut a tiny hole in it, and let the light pass through that hole onto another piece of paper. On the second piece of paper, you'll see the shadow of the Sun, but you won't be looking at it directly.

Online streaming: If you don't have special glasses or equipment to observe the eclipse, you can watch it online. Sometimes organizations livestream eclipses, so you can watch them without risking harm to your eyes.

Remember that looking directly at the Sun without proper protection can seriously harm your eyes. Always prioritize safety and use one of these methods to safely view the eclipse!"

Beliefs About Eclipse

People have had different ideas for a long time about what happens during an eclipse.

Some thought it was a sign from the gods, like in old tales.

Sometimes people believed that an eclipse could bring something bad, like illnesses or misfortunes.

Others thought it could also be something good, like a symbol of a new beginning, just as when everything starts growing again in the spring.

In some places, people did special things, like singing songs to ward off the bad effects of the eclipse.

There were also legends about animals behaving strangely during an eclipse.

Today, scientists study eclipses to learn more about the Sun and the Moon. They know that eclipses are cool phenomena in our world that can be observed, but it's essential to do so carefully to avoid harming our eyes!

Full Moons + New Moons 2024

MONTH	NEW MOON	FULL MOON
JANUARY	Jan 11 New Moon In Capricorn	Jan 25 Full Moon In Leo
FEBRUARY	Feb 9 New Moon In Aquarius	Feb 24 Full Moon In Virgo
MARCH	March 10 New Moon In Pisces	March 25 Full Moon In Libra
APRIL	April 8 New Moon In Aries	April 23 Full Moon In Scorpio
MAY	May 8 New Moon In Taurus	May 23 Full Moon In Sag
JUNE	June 6 New Moon In Gemini	June 22 Full Moon In Capricorn
JULY	July 15 New Moon In Cancer	July 21 Full Moon In Capricorn
AUGUST	Aug 4 New Moon In Leo	Aug 19 Full Moon In Aquarius
SEPTEMBER	Sept 3 New Moon In Virgo	Sept 18 Full Moon In Pisces
OCTOBER	Oct 2 New Moon In Libra	Oct 17 Full Moon In Aries
NOVEMBER	Nov 1 New Moon In Scorpio	Nov 15 Full Moon In Taurus
DECEMBER	Dec 1-new Moon In Sag Dec 30-black Moon In Cap	Dec 15 Full Moon In Gemini

Moon Calendar 2024

JANUARY

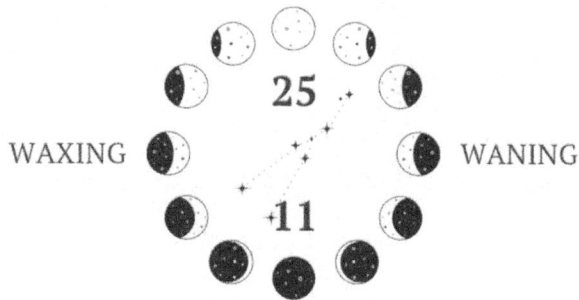

WAXING · 25 · 11 · WANING

FEBRUARY

WAXING · 24 · 9 · WANING

MARCH

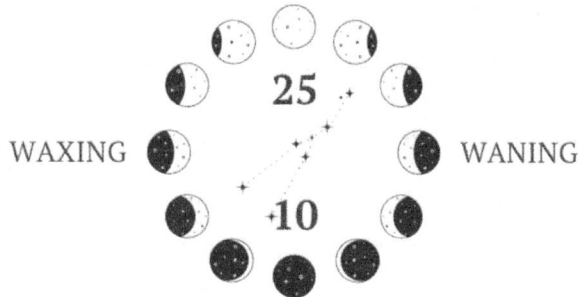

WAXING · 25 · 10 · WANING

APRIL

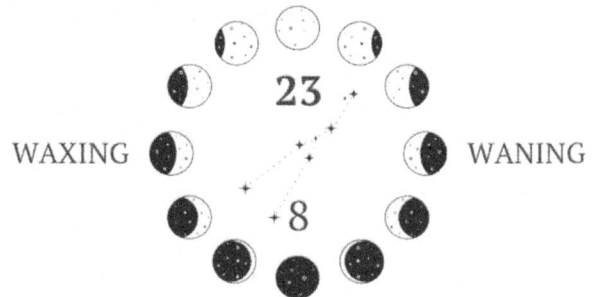

WAXING · 23 · 8 · WANING

MAY

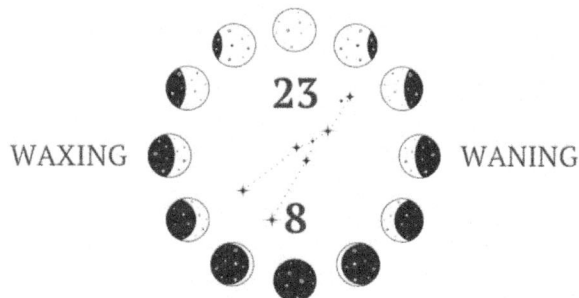

WAXING · 23 · 8 · WANING

JUNE

WAXING · 22 · 6 · WANING

Moon Calendar 2024

JULY

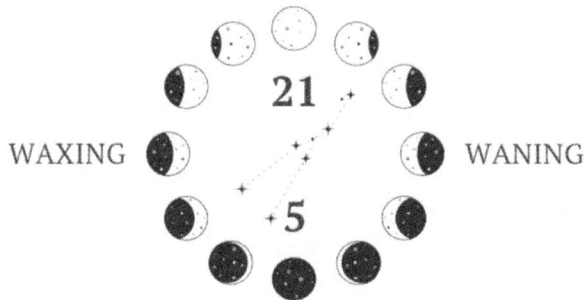

21

WAXING · WANING

5

AUGUST

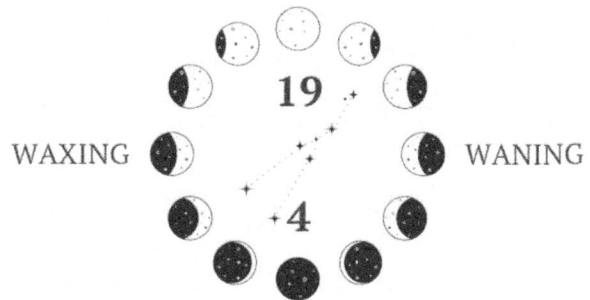

19

WAXING · WANING

4

SEPTEMBER

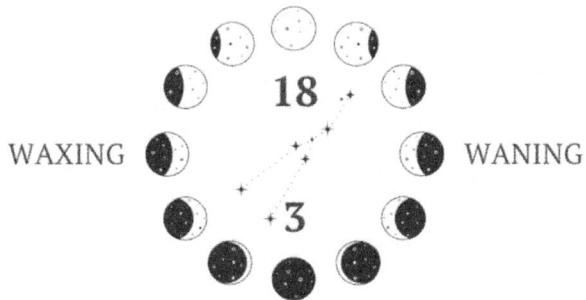

18

WAXING · WANING

3

OCTOBER

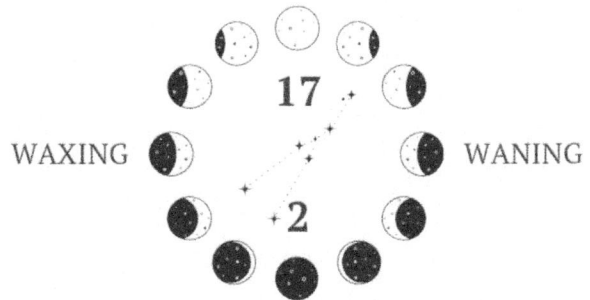

17

WAXING · WANING

2

NOVEMBER

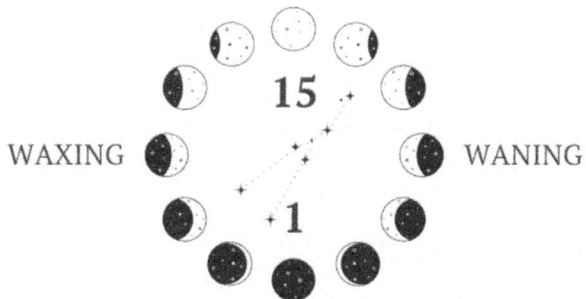

15

WAXING · WANING

1

DECEMBER

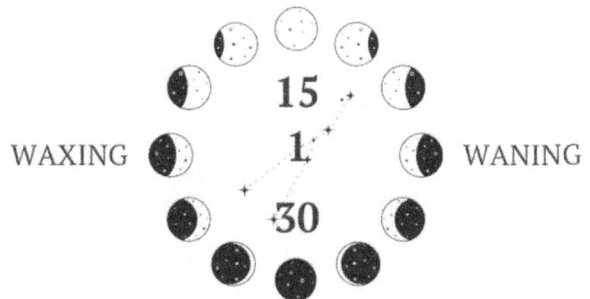

15

1

WAXING · WANING

30

COLOR
TEST
PAGE

Count the Objects #1

and Type the Result in a Square

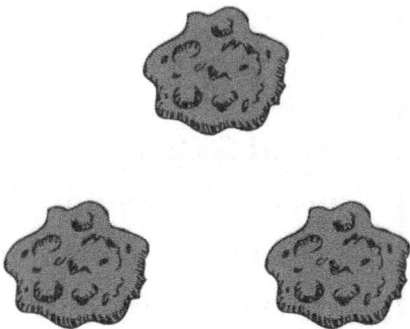

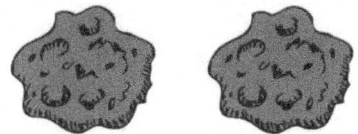

Sudoku 4x4

1

	3		1
	2		3
2		3	
3		1	

2

2	4		
	1		4
		4	2
4		3	

3

	3		4
	4		1
3		4	
4		1	

4

3			1
2	1		
	3	1	
		4	3

5

	1		4
2			1
4		1	
	2	4	

In each row, column, and small **2x2** square, you need to place numbers from **1** to **4** without repeating any of them.

Cut and Glue #1

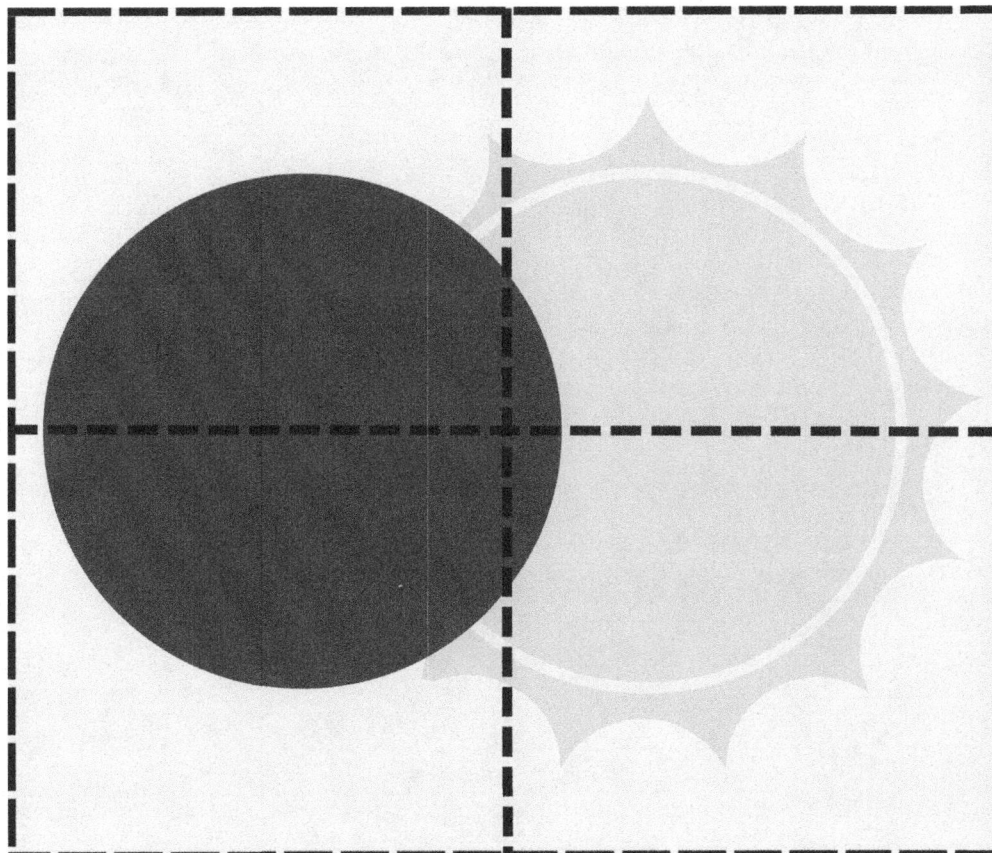

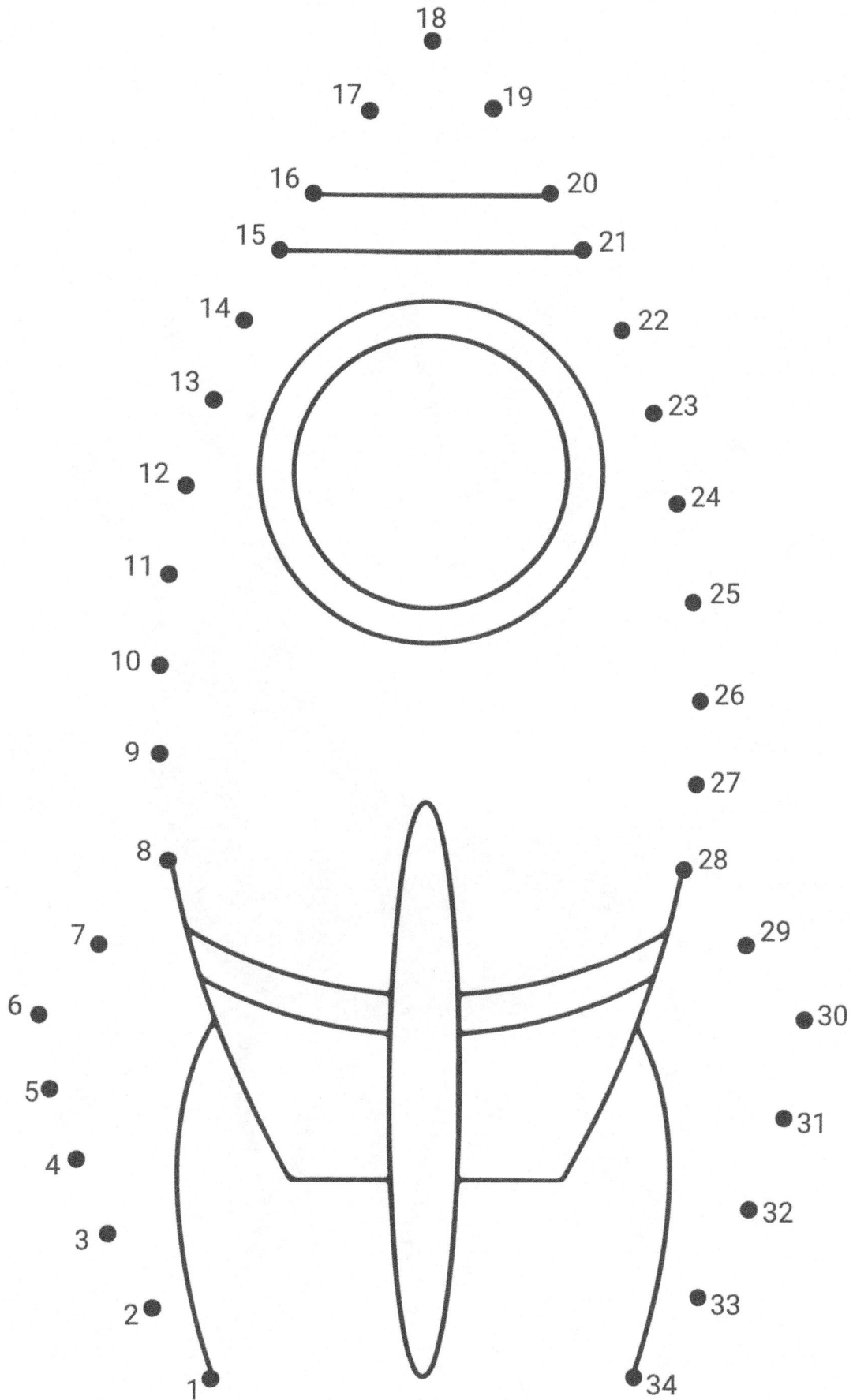

Dot to Dot #1

18

17   19

16 ———————— 20

15 ———————— 21

14   22

13   23

12   24

11   25

10   26

9   27

8   28

7   29

6   30

5   31

4   32

3   33

2

1   34

How to Draw Space #1

Your Turn!

	A	B	C	D	E	F
1						
2						
3						
4						
5						
7						
8						
9						

Maze #1

Find the way between the astronaut and the rocket according to the arrows.

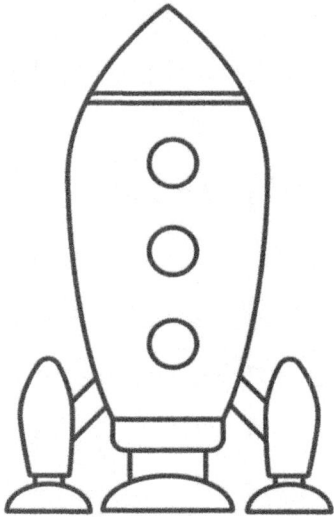

Color by Number #1

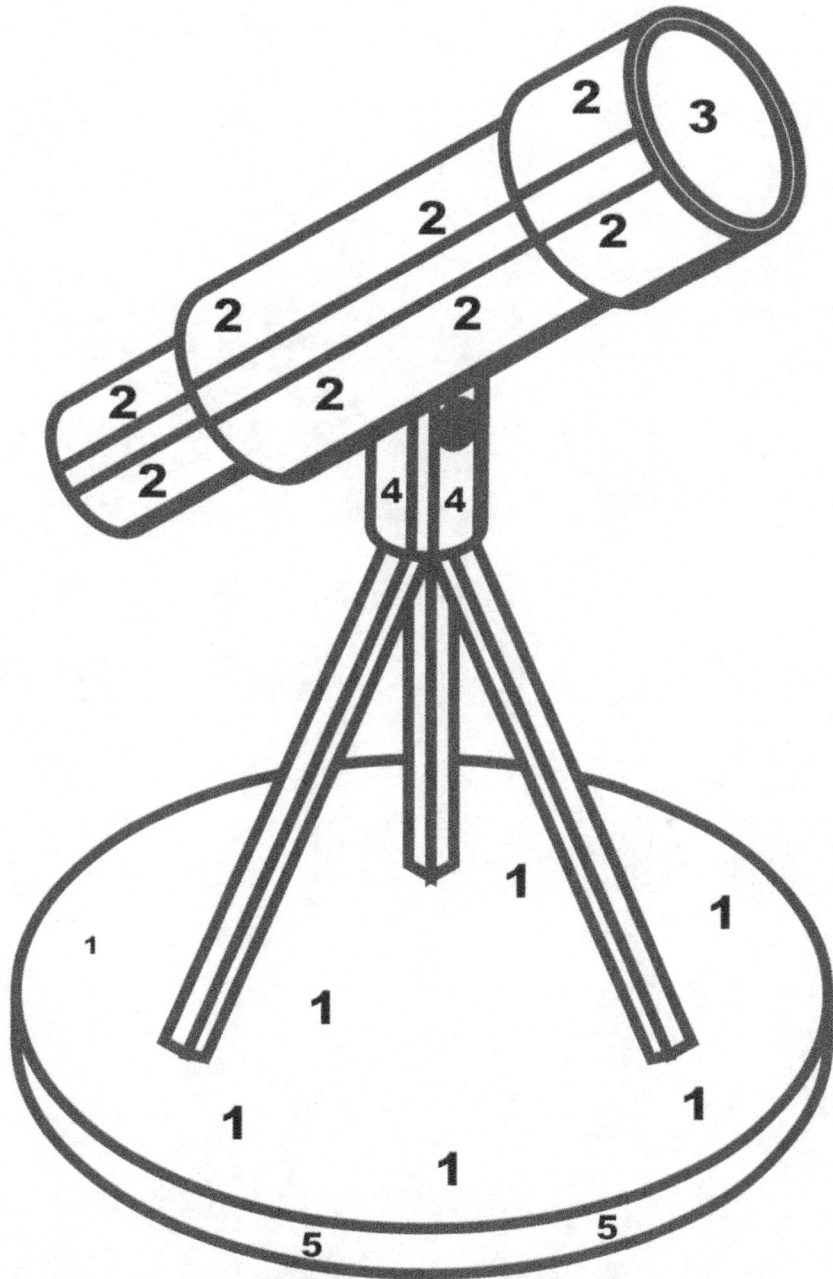

RED   PINK   LIGHT GREEN   PURPLE   MEDIUM BLUE   DARK GREEN   YELLOW   LIGHT BLUE   ORANGE

Letter is for #1

Find an Object That Is In Space.

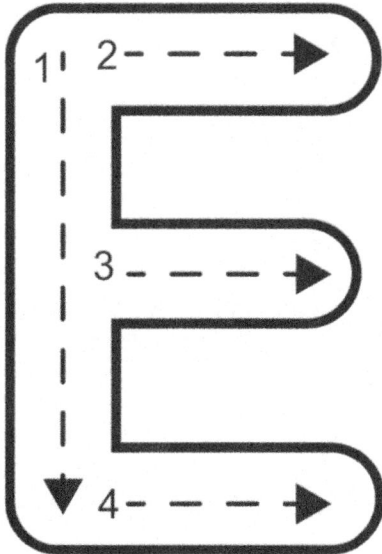

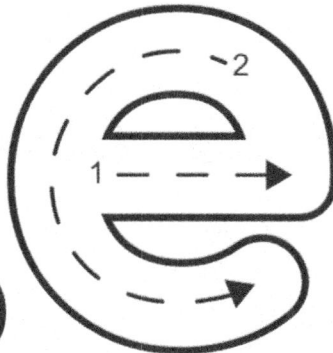

IS FOR

Egg

Elephant

Envelope

Earth

Easel

Word Search Puzzle #1

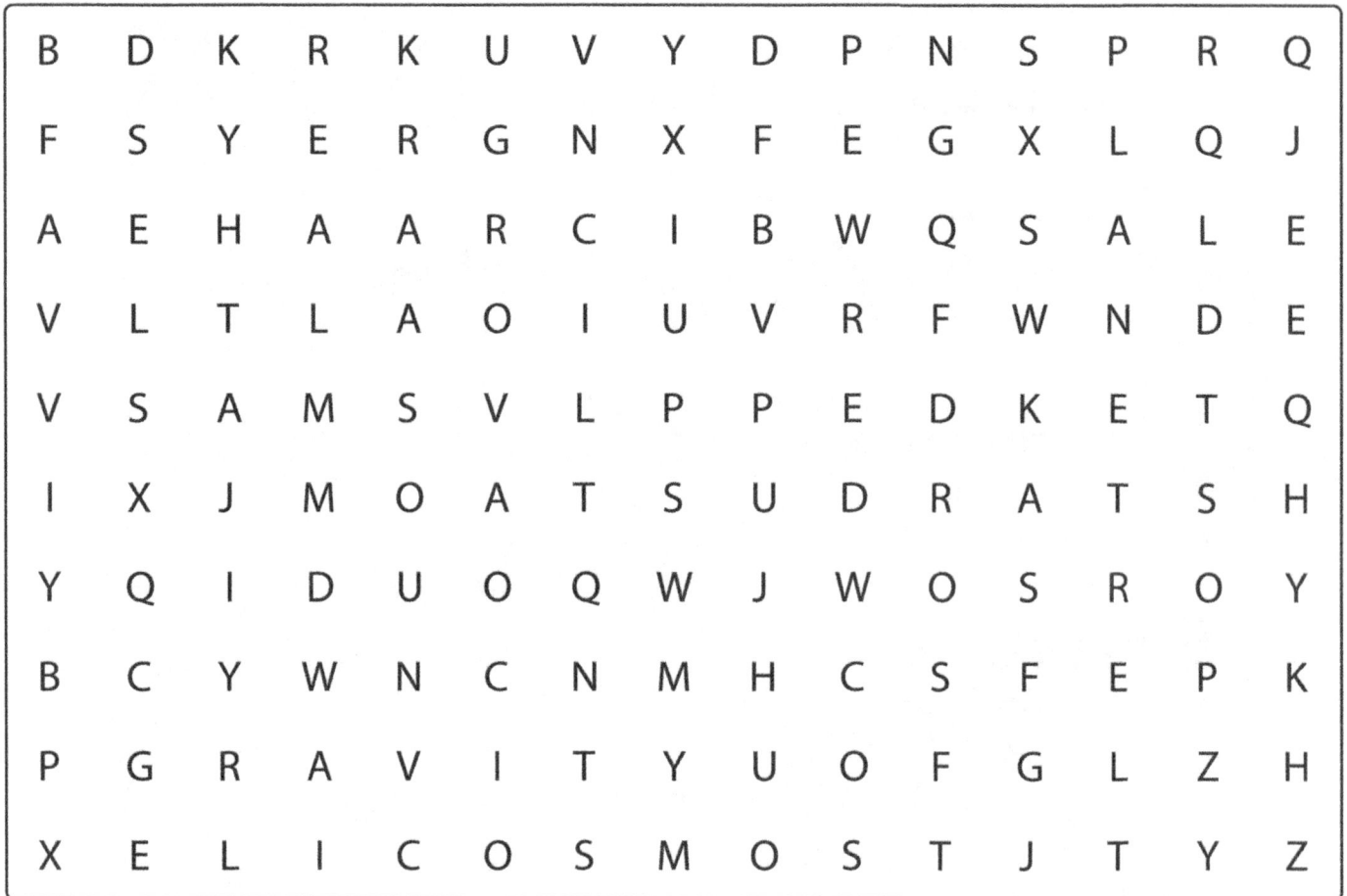

```
B D K R K U V Y D P N S P R Q
F S Y E R G N X F E G X L Q J
A E H A A R C I B W Q S A L E
V L T L A O I U V R F W N D E
V S A M S V L P P E D K E T Q
I X J M O A T S U D R A T S H
Y Q I D U O Q W J W O S R O Y
B C Y W N C N M H C S F E P K
P G R A V I T Y U O F G L Z H
X E L I C O S M O S T J T Y Z
```

COSMIC

COSMOS

GALAXY

GRAVITY

MOON

NEBULA

PLANET

STAR

STARDUST

UNIVERSE

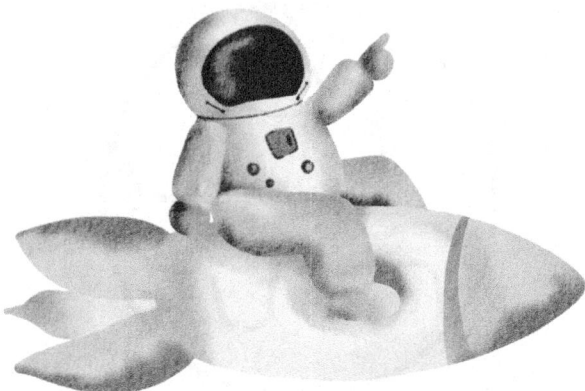

Search for hidden words in the grid of letters. Once you find the first letter of a word, follow its direction to locate the remaining letters of that word. When you find all the letters of the word, mark or underline them to know that you've found it.

Count the Objects #2

and Type the Result in a Square

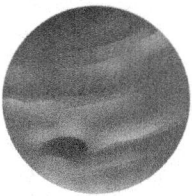

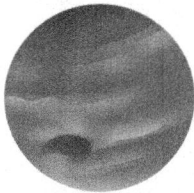

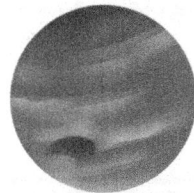

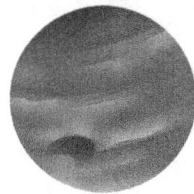

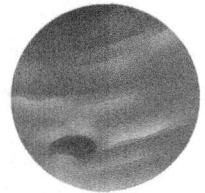

Sudoku 6x6

1

	4	3	2		1
1		6		3	
	1			5	6
	6		1		4
6	3		5	1	
2			1	6	

2

	2	4		3	
3			2	1	
2		5	1		3
		3		2	5
	3	2	6		1
4	6			5	

3

2				4	1
	5		2	3	6
3		5	6		
6			4		3
	6	3	1		
1	2	4		6	

4

1			6	4	5
	5	4	1		
5				2	3
		2	5	1	
	6			5	4
4	3	5			1

5

	3	4			6
		5		4	3
	2		4		1
4	5		3	6	
6			3	2	
5	1			6	3

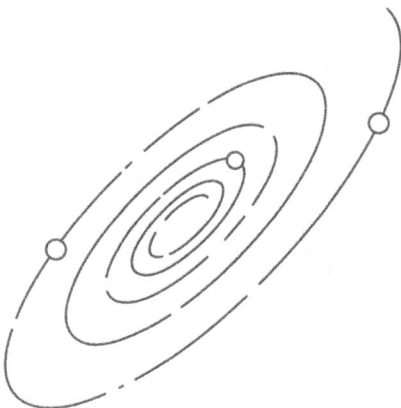

In each row, column, and small 3x3 square, you need to place numbers from 1 to 4 without repeating any of them.

Cut and Glue #2

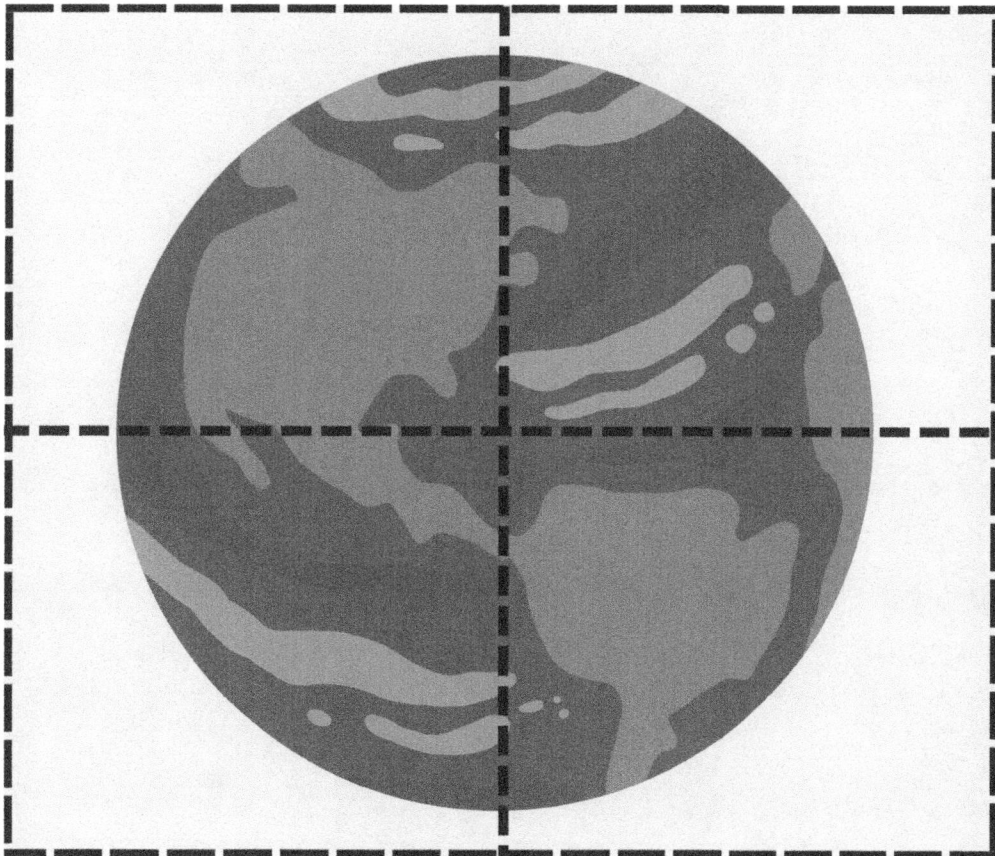

Dot to Dot #2

1

•30

•29

2•

3•

•28

27

•26

4•

•24

23•

5•

9•

•22

•21

6•   8•

•10   •25

•11   •20

•13   •19

7•   •12   •15 •17   •18

•14   •16

How to Draw Space #2

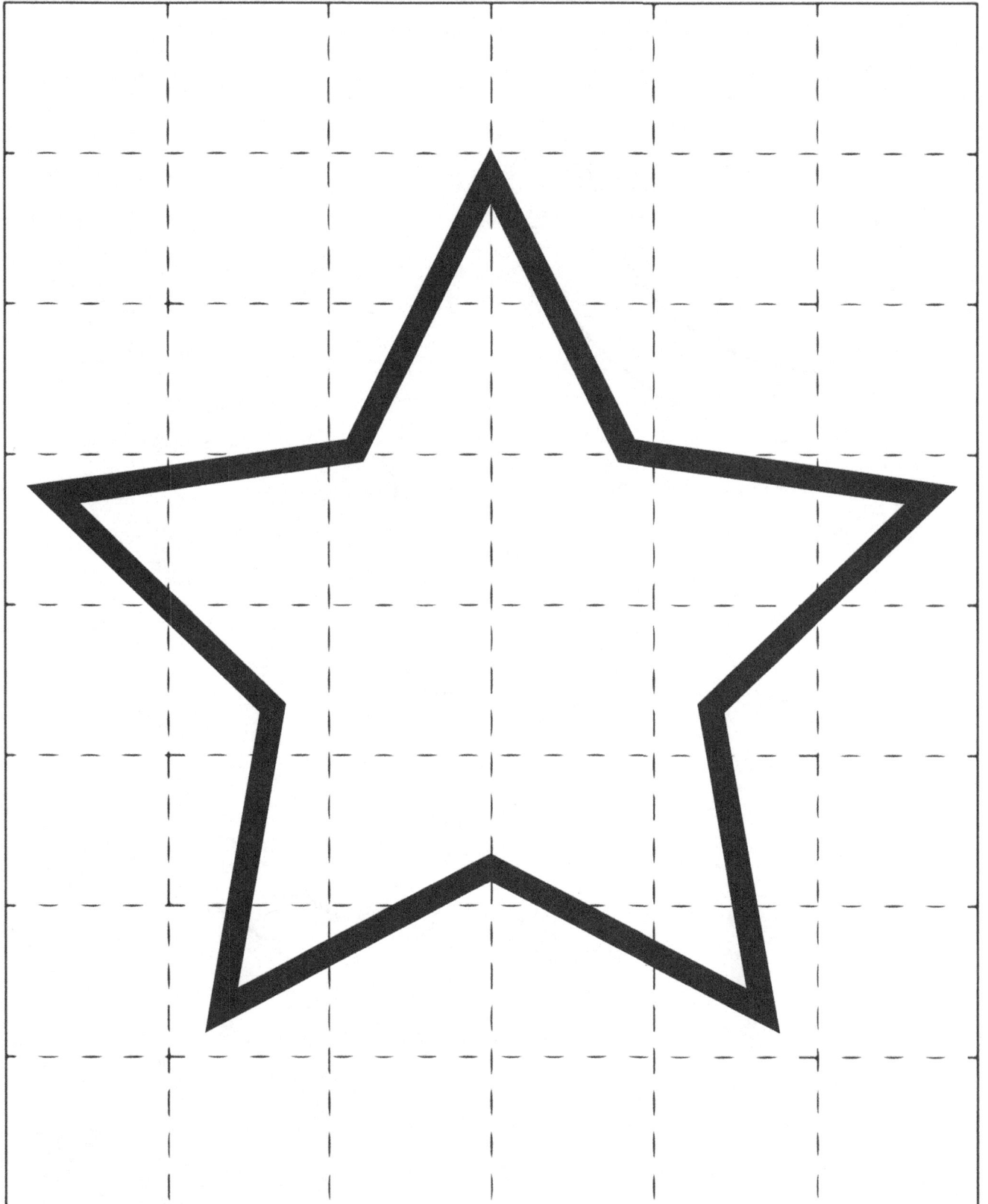

YOUR TURN!

	A	B	C	D	E	F
1						
2						
3						
4						
5						
7						
8						
9						

Maze #2

Find the way between the astronaut and the rocket according to the arrows.

Color by Number #2

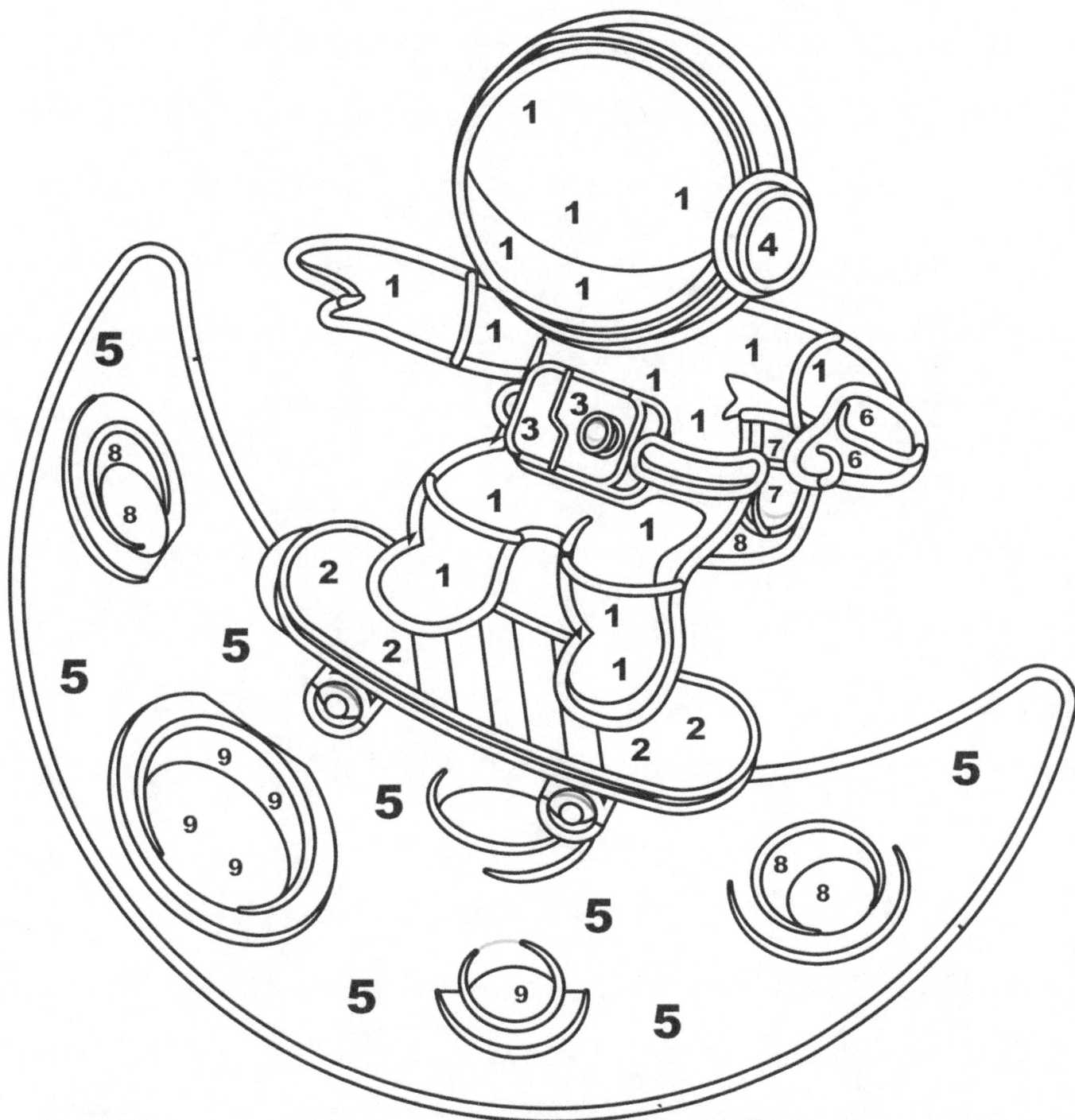

1	2	3	4	5	6	7	8	9
NAVY	YELLOW	PURPLE	LIGHT GREEN	DARK GREEN	LIGHT BLUE	RED	PINK	MEDIUM BLUE

Letter is for #2

Find an Object That Is In Space.

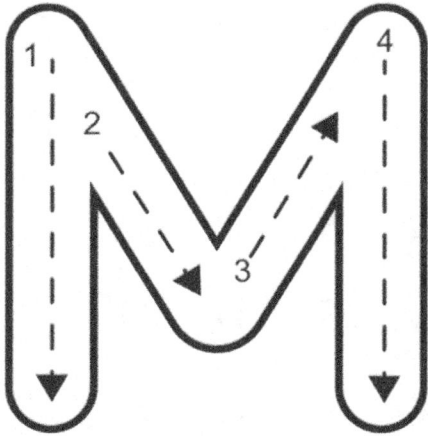 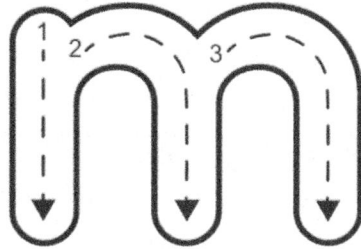

IS FOR

Mushroom

Monster

Moon

Mountains

Monkey

Word Search Puzzle #2

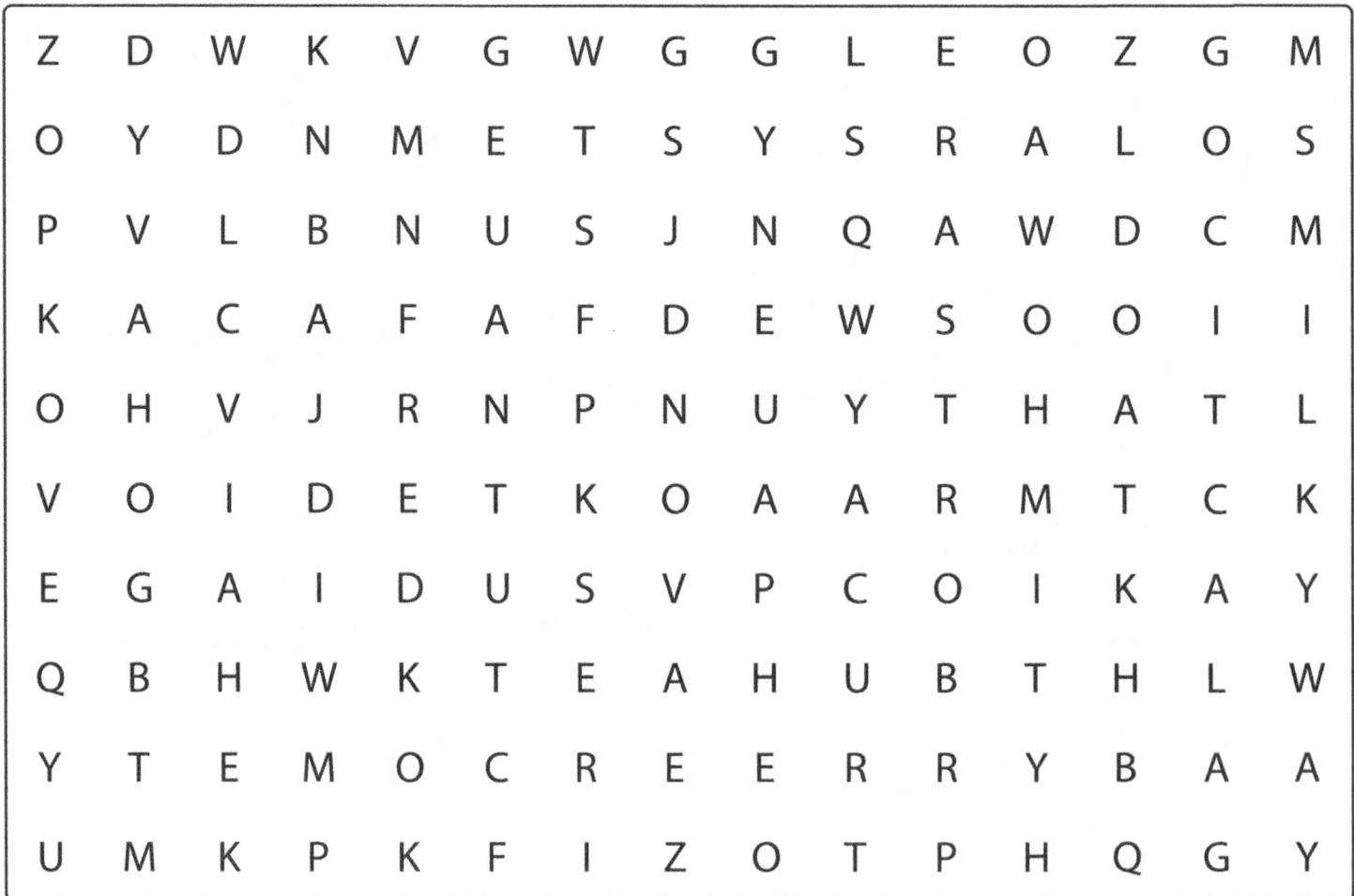

```
Z  D  W  K  V  G  W  G  G  L  E  O  Z  G  M
O  Y  D  N  M  E  T  S  Y  S  R  A  L  O  S
P  V  L  B  N  U  S  J  N  Q  A  W  D  C  M
K  A  C  A  F  A  F  D  E  W  S  O  O  I  I
O  H  V  J  R  N  P  N  U  Y  T  H  A  T  L
V  O  I  D  E  T  K  O  A  A  R  M  T  C  K
E  G  A  I  D  U  S  V  P  C  O  I  K  A  Y
Q  B  H  W  K  T  E  A  H  U  B  T  H  L  W
Y  T  E  M  O  C  R  E  E  R  R  Y  B  A  A
U  M  K  P  K  F  I  Z  O  T  P  H  Q  G  Y
```

ASTRAL   MILKY WAY   SUN
ASTRO   NOVA   VOID
COMET   ORBIT
GALACTIC   SOLAR SYSTEM

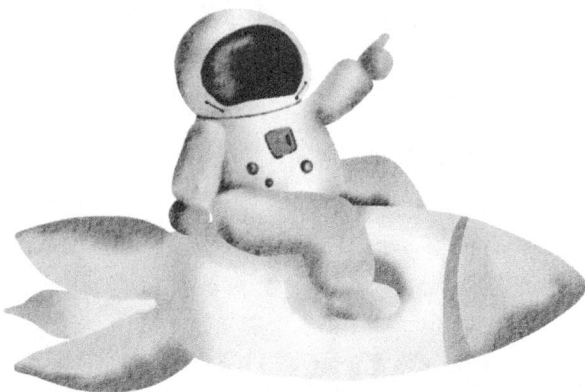

Search for hidden words in the grid of letters. Once you find the first letter of a word, follow its direction to locate the remaining letters of that word. When you find all the letters of the word, mark or underline them to know that you've found it.

Count the Objects #3

and Type the Result in a Square

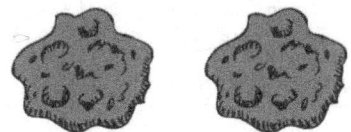

Sudoku 4x4

6

4		2	
	3	1	
1			2
	2		1

7

1	3		
	4	3	
3			4
		2	3

8

1			3
	4	1	
	1		4
4		2	

9

3	1		
	4	1	
1			2
		3	1

10

1			3
	3		4
4		3	
	1	4	

In each row, column, and small 2x2 square, you need to place numbers from 1 to 4 without repeating any of them.

Cut and Glue #3

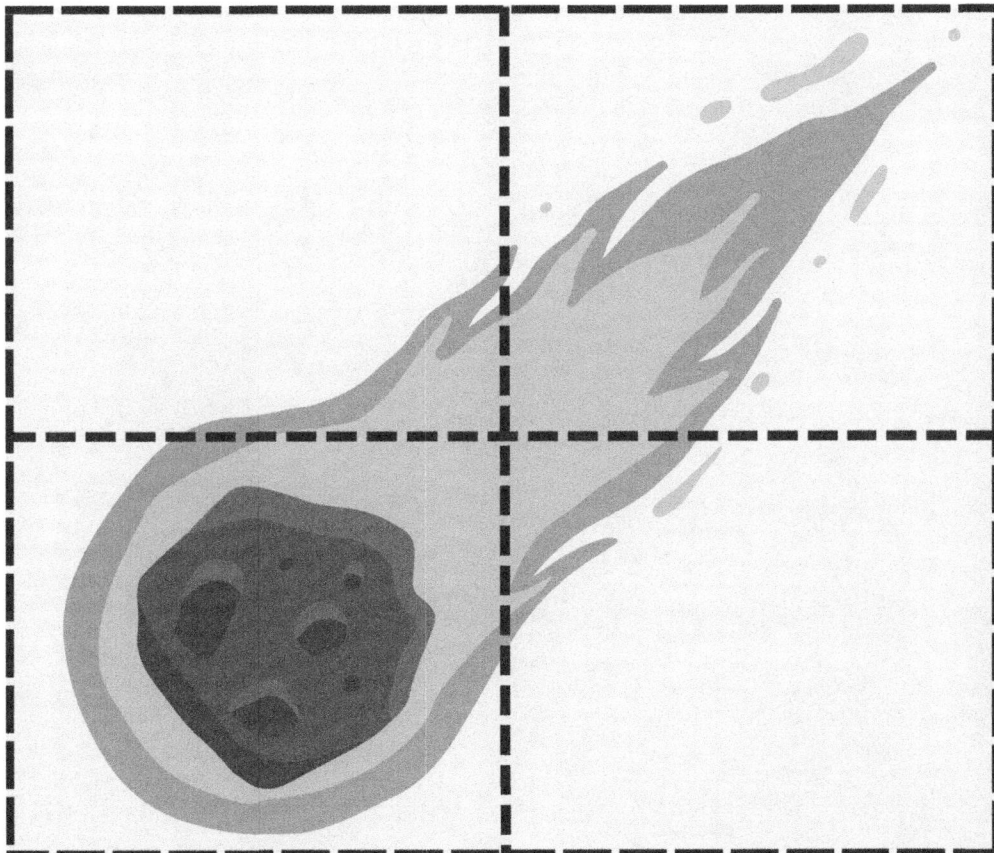

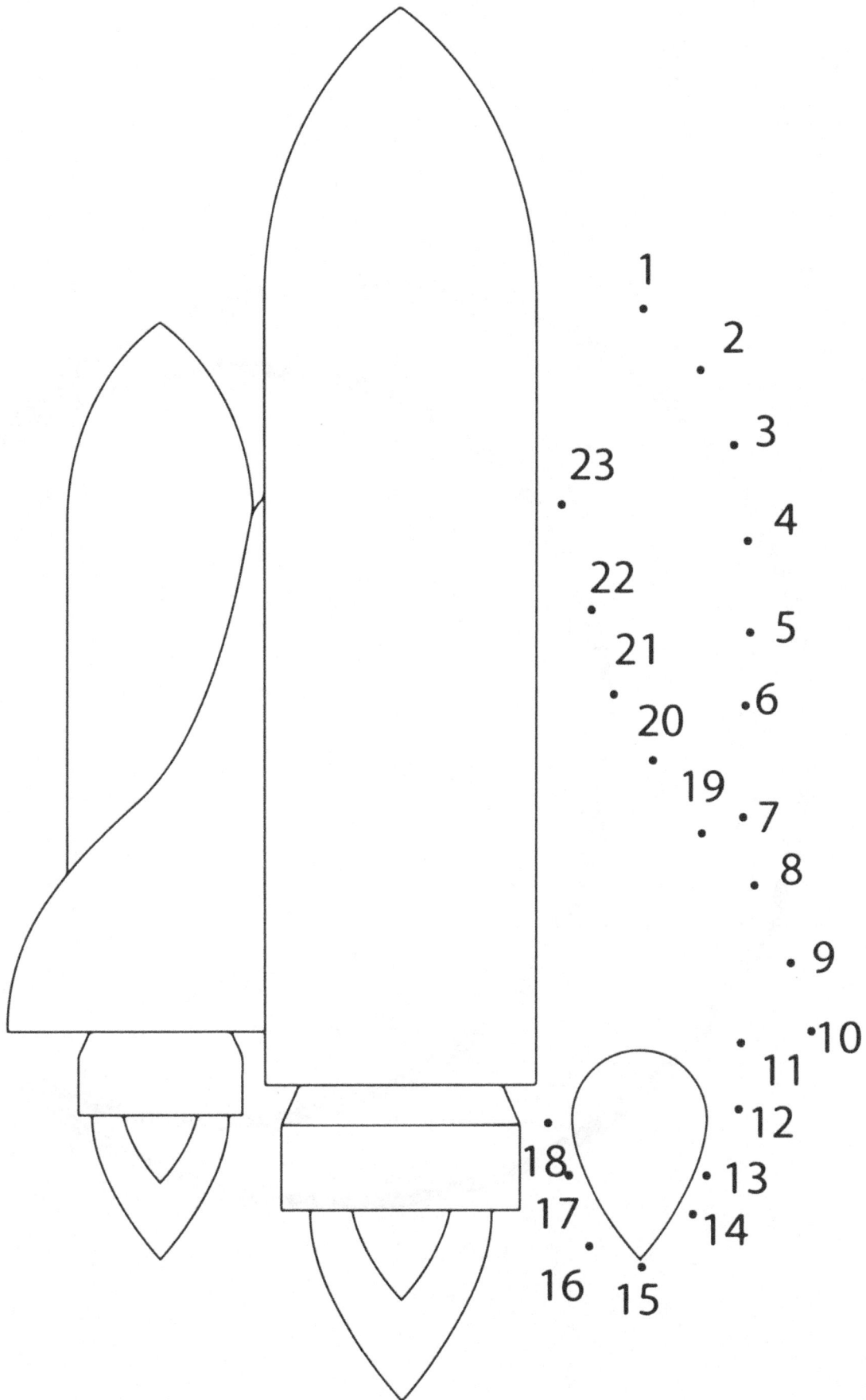

Dot to Dot #3

1
2
3
23
4
22
21
5
20
6
19
7
8
9
10
11
12
18
13
17
14
16
15

How to Draw Space #3

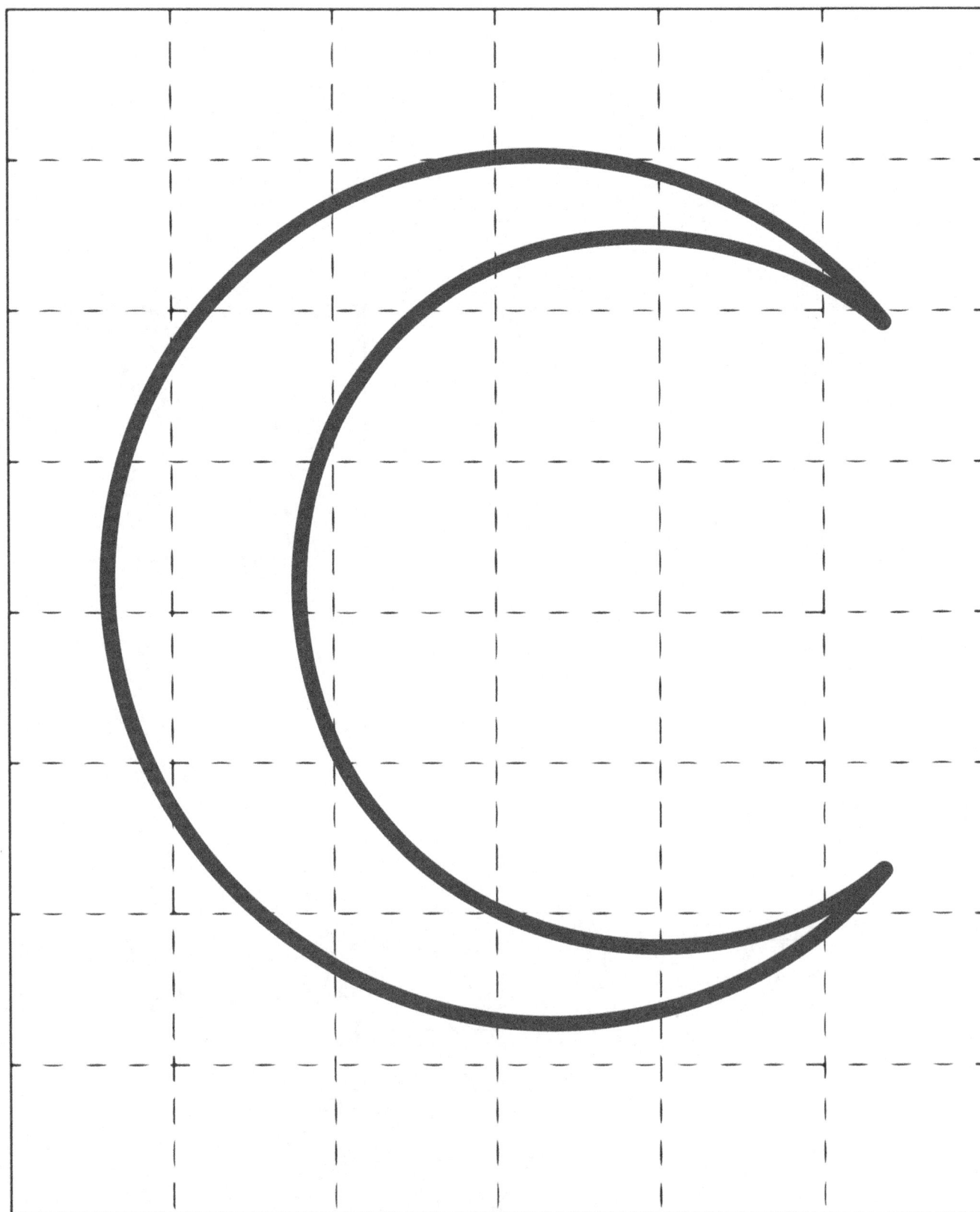

YOUR TURN!

	A	B	C	D	E	F
1						
2						
3						
4						
5						
7						
8						
9						

Find a way to earth

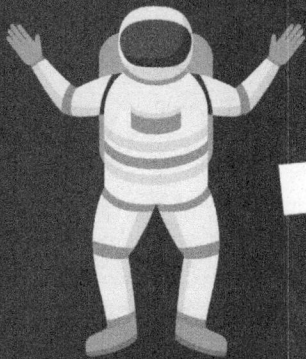

Color by Number #3

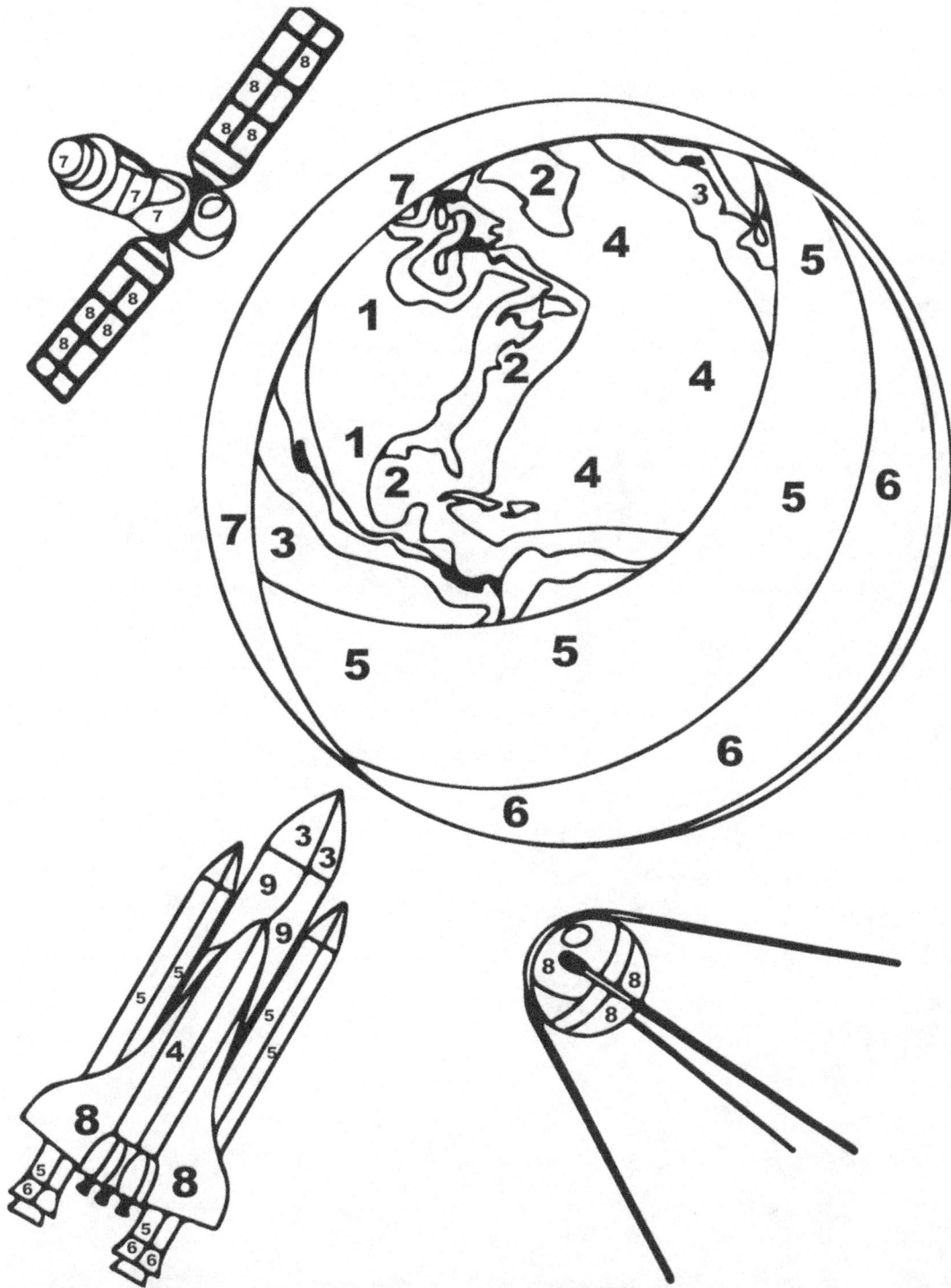

RED 1 PINK 2 LIGHT GREEN 3 PURPLE 4 MEDIUM BLUE 5 DARK GREEN 6 YELLOW 7 LIGHT BLUE 8 ORANGE 9

Letter is for #3

Find an Object That Is In Space.

IS FOR

Robot

Rain

Rocket

Rainbow

Radio

Find the Difference

Find **12** differences
between these pictures.

Count the Objects #4

and Type the Result in a Square

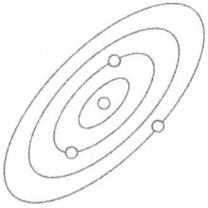

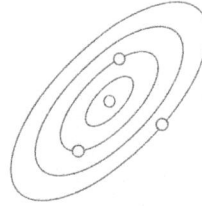

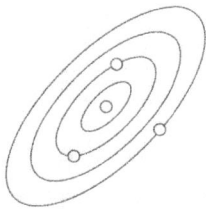

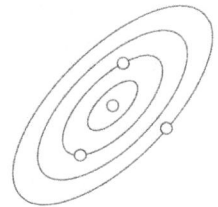

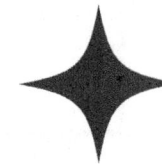

Sudoku 6x6

6

3	5			2	
6		1			5
	3		4	1	6
4	1	6			
		5	1		3
		3	2	5	4

7

3		5	4		
	1			5	6
6	5		2		
		3	1	6	5
1		6		2	
5	2			3	1

8

1	3			6	2
		2	4	1	3
	1			4	5
4	5	6			
			2	5	6
6		5	1		

9

1		4		5	
	6		3	4	
3	5				2
		2	5	1	3
5		3		2	4
	2	6	1		

10

	1	4		5	
6			1		4
	3		5	2	1
1	2	5			6
	4		2	6	
2		3			5

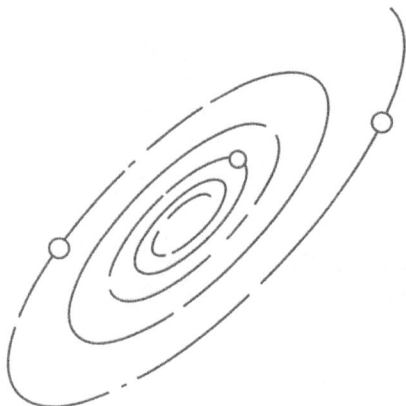

In each row, column, and small 3x3 square, you need to place numbers from 1 to 4 without repeating any of them.

Cut and Glue #4

Dot to Dot #4

Picture Brainiac

15 14
16   13
17   12
18   11
19
20   10

                                9

                                8

                                7

                                6

                            5

                        4

                    3

                2

            1

How to Draw Space #4

YOUR TURN!

	A	B	C	D	E	F
1						
2						
3						
4						
5						
7						
8						
9						

Maze #3

Find the way between the astronaut and the rocket according to the arrows.

Color by Number #4

1	2	3	4	5	6	7	8	9
PURPLE	RED	LIGHT GREEN	PINK	NAVY	YELLOW	LIGHT BLUE	DARK GREEN	DARK PINK

Letter is for #4

Find an Object That Is In Space.

IS FOR

Sloth

Snail

Spider

Squirrel

Satellite

Word Search Puzzle #3

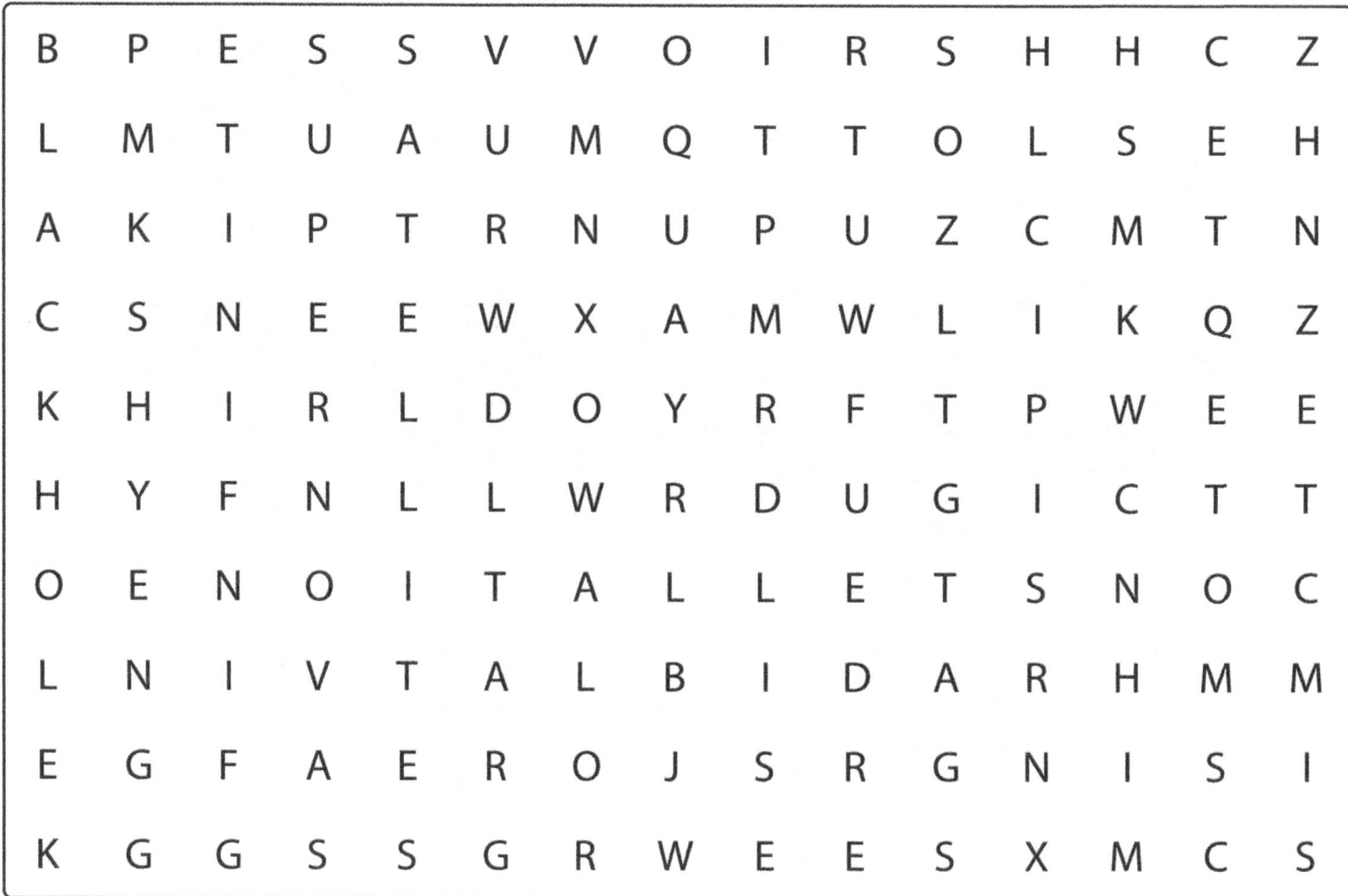

B	P	E	S	S	V	V	O	I	R	S	H	H	C	Z
L	M	T	U	A	U	M	Q	T	T	O	L	S	E	H
A	K	I	P	T	R	N	U	P	U	Z	C	M	T	N
C	S	N	E	E	W	X	A	M	W	L	I	K	Q	Z
K	H	I	R	L	D	O	Y	R	F	T	P	W	E	E
H	Y	F	N	L	L	W	R	D	U	G	I	C	T	T
O	E	N	O	I	T	A	L	L	E	T	S	N	O	C
L	N	I	V	T	A	L	B	I	D	A	R	H	M	M
E	G	F	A	E	R	O	J	S	R	G	N	I	S	I
K	G	G	S	S	G	R	W	E	E	S	X	M	C	S

BLACK HOLE
CONSTELLATION
INFINITE
PLUTO

ROCKET
SATELLITES
SUPERNOVA
TIME

URANUS
WORLD

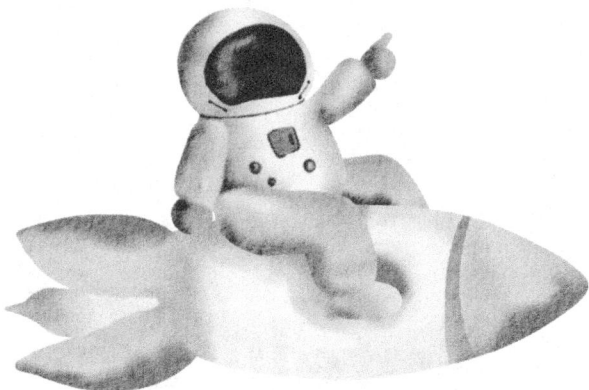

Search for hidden words in the grid of letters.
Once you find the first letter of a word, follow its
direction to locate the remaining letters of that
word. When you find all the letters of the word,
mark or underline them to know that you've
found it.

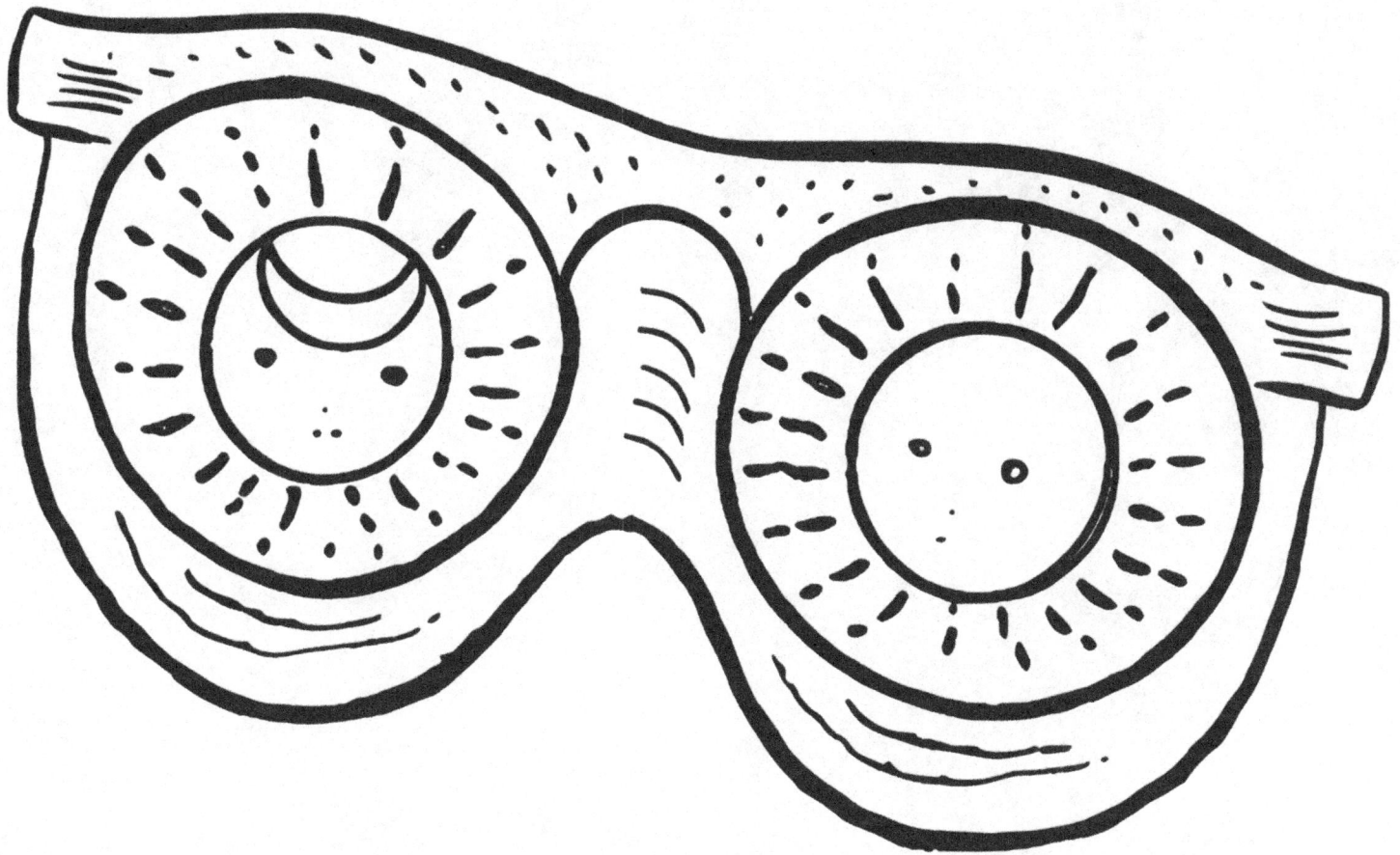

Count the Objects #5

and Type the Result in a Square

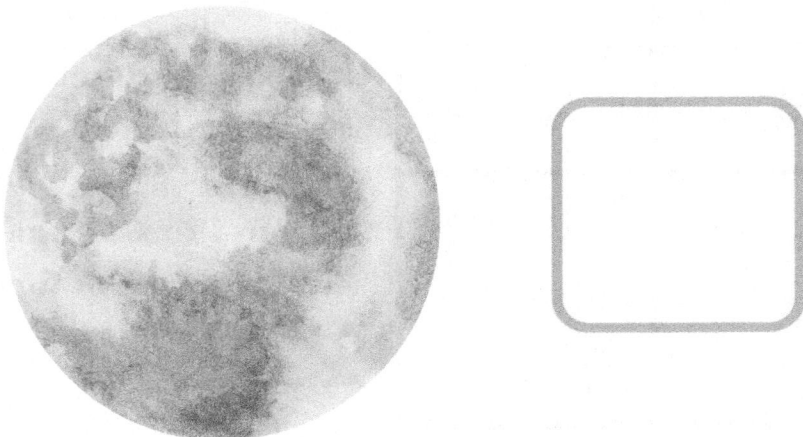

Sudoku 4x4

11

	2		1
3		2	
	4	1	
1			2

12

4			3
2			1
	4	3	
	2	1	

13

1		2	
4		1	
	1		2
	4		1

14

	1	4	
4			1
	4		2
1		3	

15

	2	4	
1			2
	1		3
2		1	

In each row, column, and small 2x2 square, you need to place numbers from 1 to 4 without repeating any of them.

Cut and Glue #5

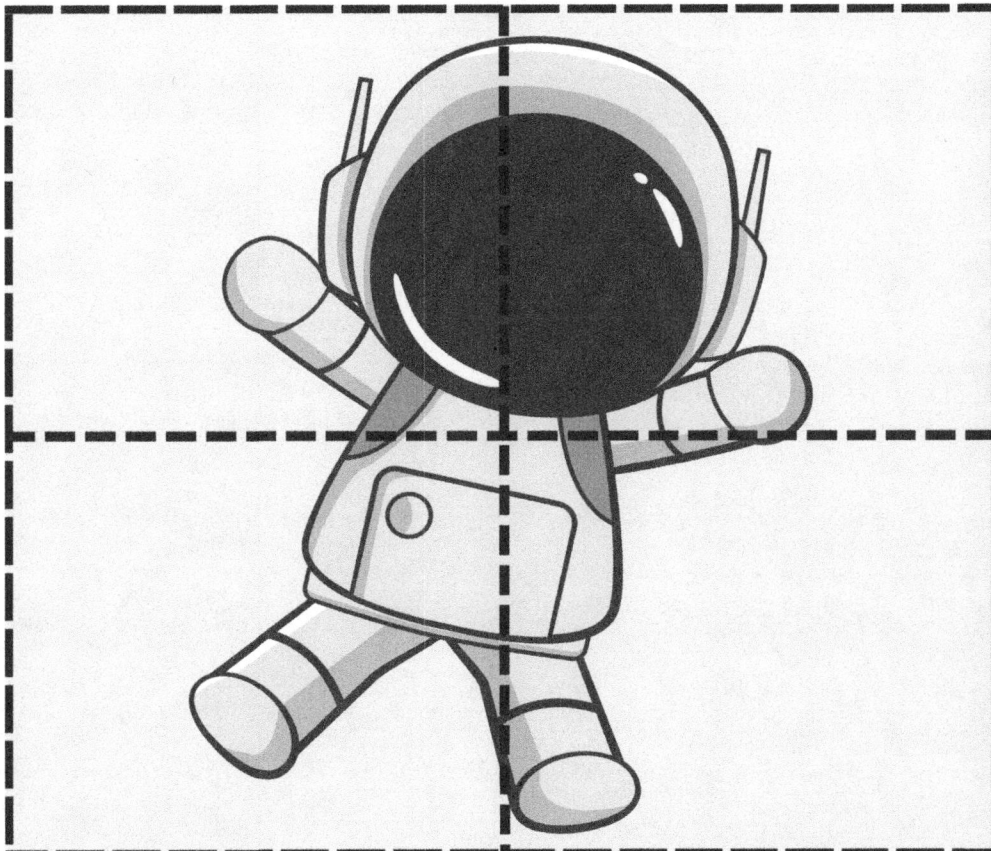

Dot to Dot #5

How to Draw Space #5

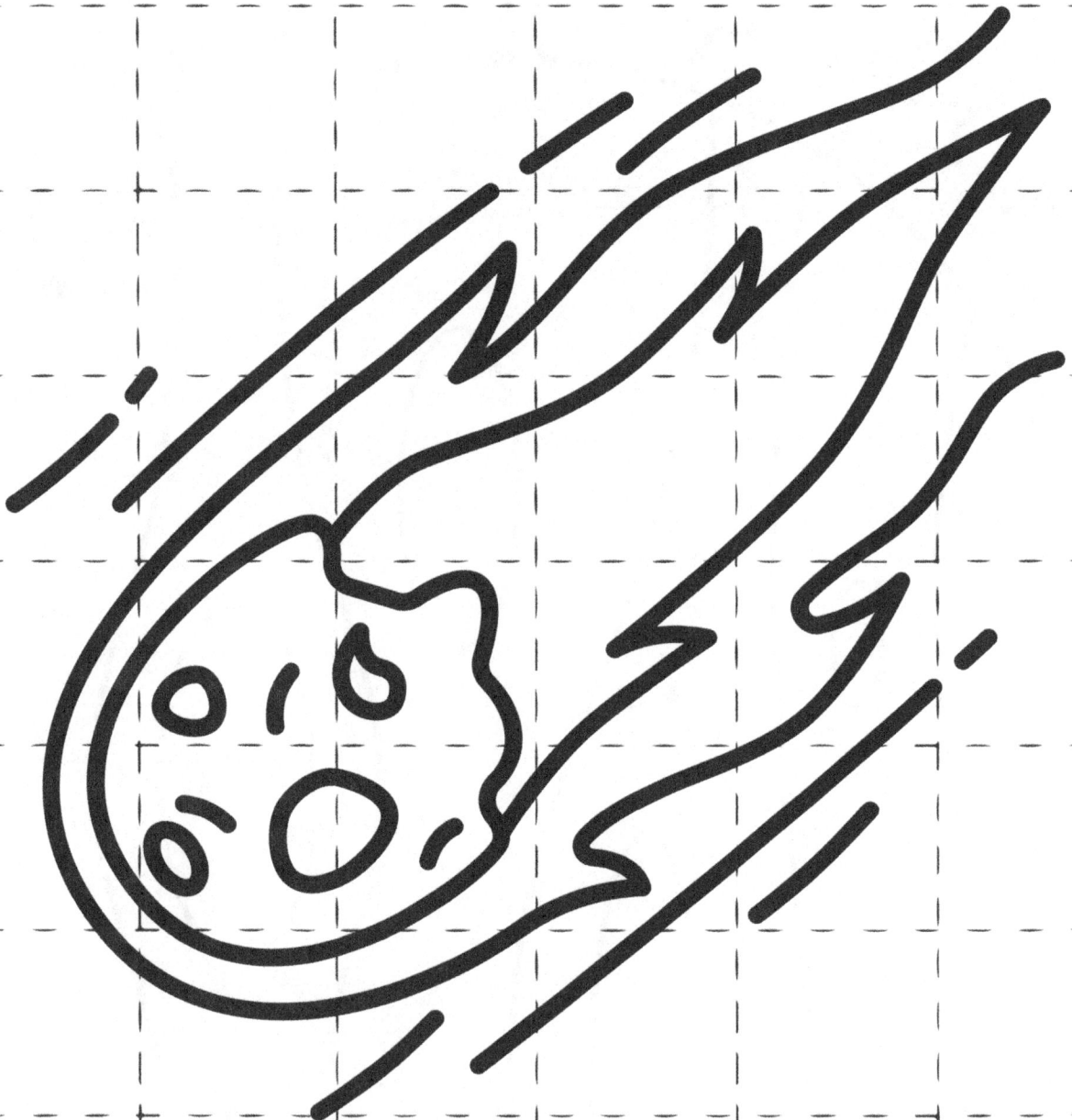

YOUR TURN!

	A	B	C	D	E	F
1						
2						
3						
4						
5						
7						
8						
9						

Maze #4

Find the way between the astronaut and the rocket according to the arrows.

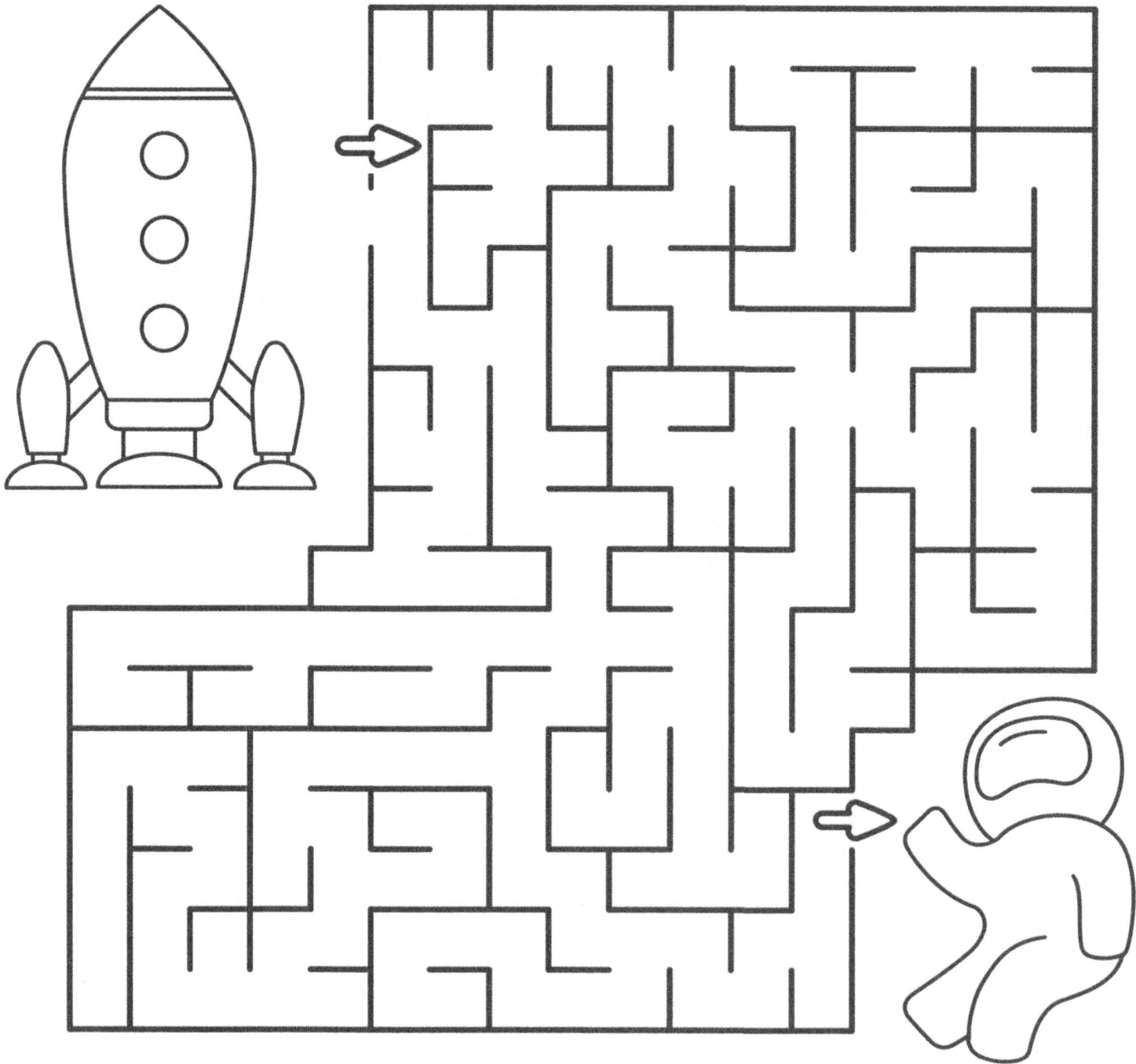

Color by Number #5

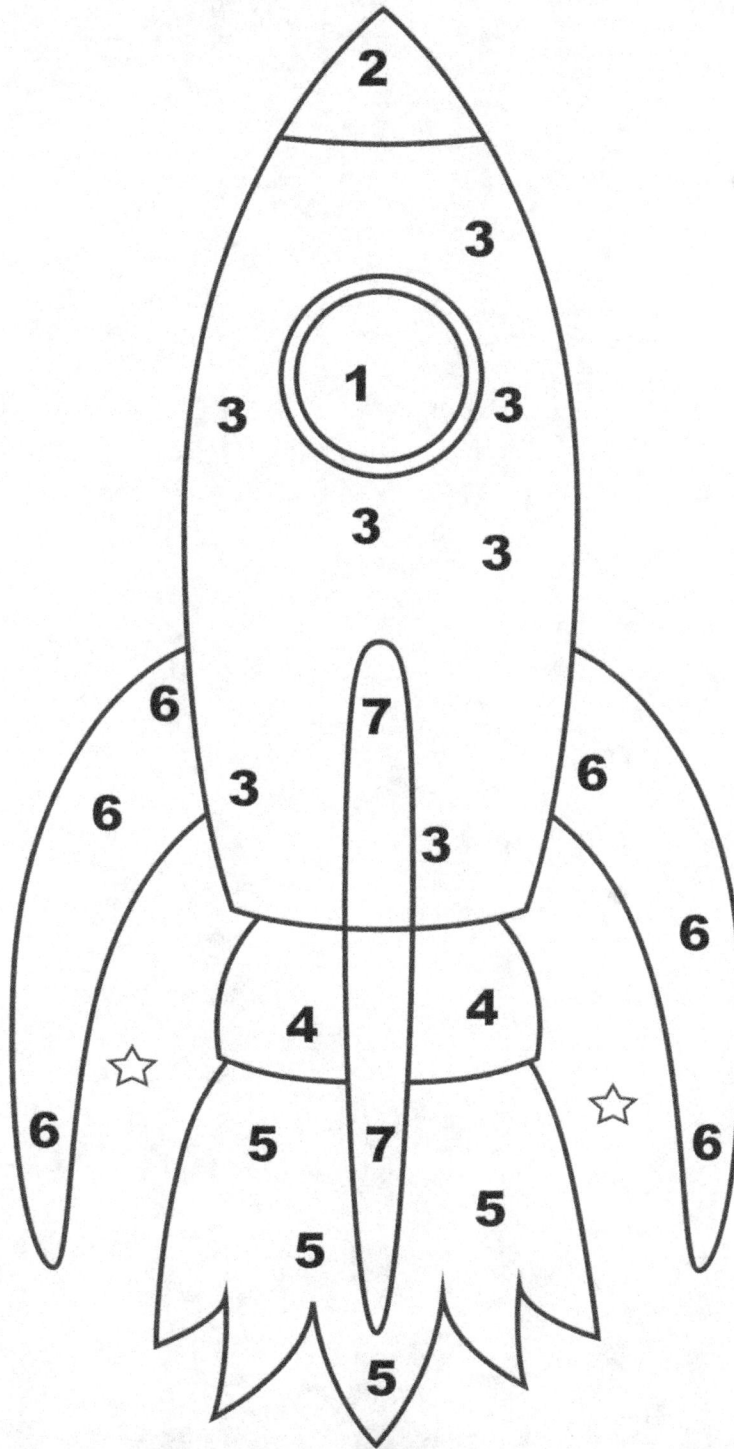

1	2	3	4	5	6	7	8	9
DARK PINK	RED	LIGHT GREEN	PINK	NAVY	YELLOW	LIGHT BLUE	DARK GREEN	PURPLE

Letter is for #5

Find an Object That Is In Space.

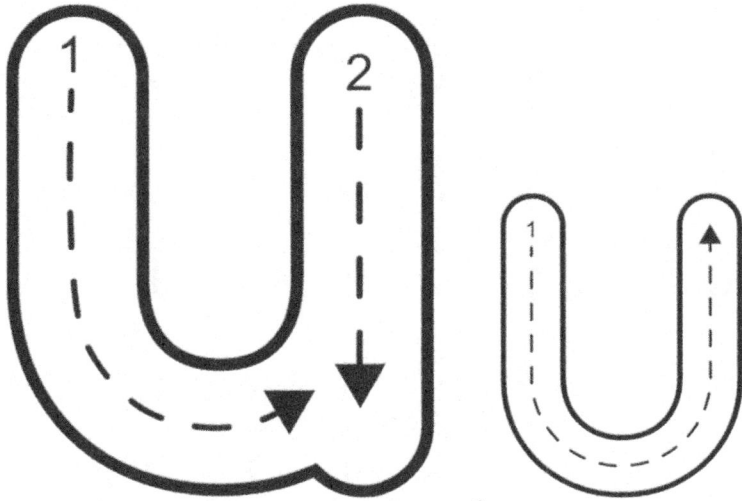

IS FOR

Unicycle

Umbrella

Unicorn

UFO

Word Search Puzzle #4

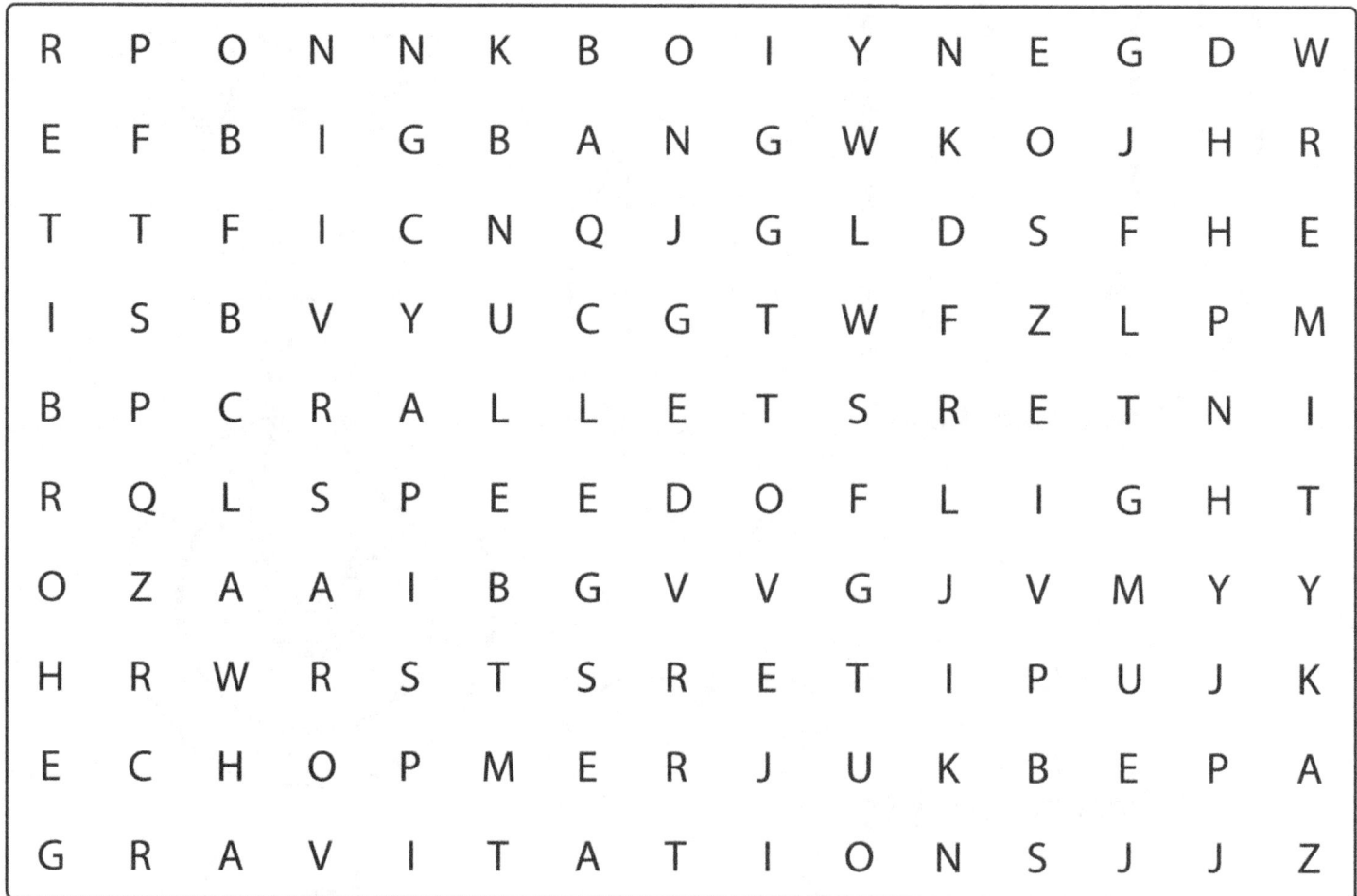

R	P	O	N	N	K	B	O	I	Y	N	E	G	D	W
E	F	B	I	G	B	A	N	G	W	K	O	J	H	R
T	T	F	I	C	N	Q	J	G	L	D	S	F	H	E
I	S	B	V	Y	U	C	G	T	W	F	Z	L	P	M
B	P	C	R	A	L	L	E	T	S	R	E	T	N	I
R	Q	L	S	P	E	E	D	O	F	L	I	G	H	T
O	Z	A	A	I	B	G	V	V	G	J	V	M	Y	Y
H	R	W	R	S	T	S	R	E	T	I	P	U	J	K
E	C	H	O	P	M	E	R	J	U	K	B	E	P	A
G	R	A	V	I	T	A	T	I	O	N	S	J	J	Z

BIG BANG   JUPITER   SKY

ECHO   ORBITER   SPEED OF LIGHT

GRAVITATION   PLASMA

INTERSTELLAR   QUASAR

Search for hidden words in the grid of letters. Once you find the first letter of a word, follow its direction to locate the remaining letters of that word. When you find all the letters of the word, mark or underline them to know that you've found it.

Count the Objects #6

and Type the Result in a Square

Sudoku 6x6

11

		6	2	4	
4		2		3	
2	3			5	1
5		1	3		4
	2		4	6	
6	4				2

12

2	1			5	
	3	5		4	2
4			2	3	
3		2	6		
	4		5		3
	2	3		6	1

13

5		6	1	4	
3	4		5		
	5	4		3	
2	1				4
		5		2	6
	6	2	3		5

14

	3	2	5		4
4			1	2	3
	6	5			1
2			3	5	
5		4			2
	2		4	1	

15

3	2	6			
4		1		6	
		4	3	5	2
2	3		1	4	
	1	3			4
			5	3	1

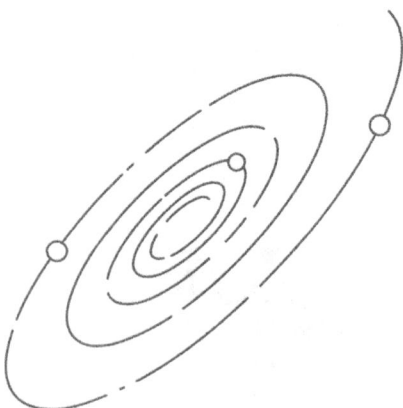

In each row, column, and small 3x3 square, you need to place numbers from 1 to 4 without repeating any of them.

Solutions

Maze #1

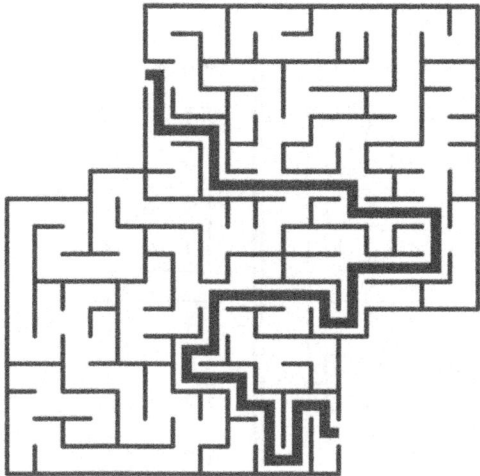

Maze #2

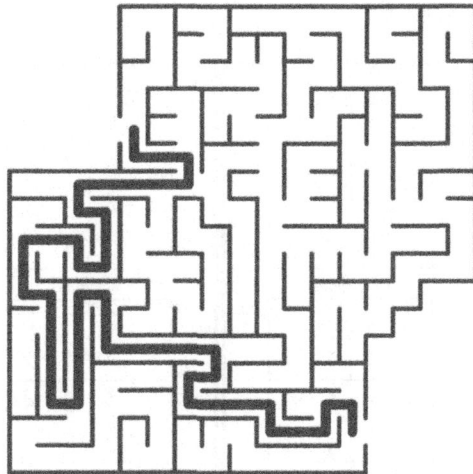

Maze #3

Maze #4

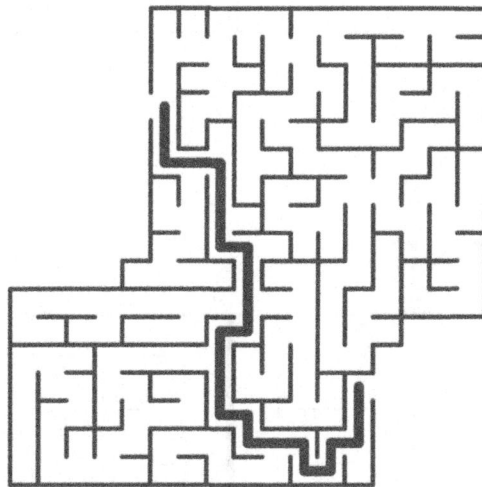

Find a way to earth

Solutions

Sudoku 4x4

1 (SOLUTIONS)

4	3	2	1
1	2	4	3
2	1	3	4
3	4	1	2

2 (SOLUTIONS)

2	4	1	3
3	1	2	4
1	3	4	2
4	2	3	1

6 (SOLUTIONS)

4	1	2	3
2	3	1	4
1	4	3	2
3	2	4	1

7 (SOLUTIONS)

1	3	4	2
2	4	3	1
3	2	1	4
4	1	2	3

11 (SOLUTIONS)

4	2	3	1
3	1	2	4
2	4	1	3
1	3	4	2

12 (SOLUTIONS)

4	1	2	3
2	3	4	1
1	4	3	2
3	2	1	4

3 (SOLUTIONS)

1	3	2	4
2	4	3	1
3	1	4	2
4	2	1	3

4 (SOLUTIONS)

3	4	2	1
2	1	3	4
4	3	1	2
1	2	4	3

8 (SOLUTIONS)

1	2	4	3
3	4	1	2
2	1	3	4
4	3	2	1

9 (SOLUTIONS)

3	1	2	4
2	4	1	3
1	3	4	2
4	2	3	1

13 (SOLUTIONS)

1	3	2	4
4	2	1	3
3	1	4	2
2	4	3	1

14 (SOLUTIONS)

2	1	4	3
4	3	2	1
3	4	1	2
1	2	3	4

5 (SOLUTIONS)

3	1	2	4
2	4	3	1
4	3	1	2
1	2	4	3

10 (SOLUTIONS)

1	4	2	3
2	3	1	4
4	2	3	1
3	1	4	2

15 (SOLUTIONS)

3	2	4	1
1	4	3	2
4	1	2	3
2	3	1	4

Sudoku 6x6

1 (SOLUTIONS)

5	4	3	2	6	1
1	2	6	4	3	5
4	1	2	3	5	6
3	6	5	1	2	4
6	3	4	5	1	2
2	5	1	6	4	3

2 (SOLUTIONS)

1	2	4	5	3	6
3	5	6	2	1	4
2	4	5	1	6	3
6	1	3	4	2	5
5	3	2	6	4	1
4	6	1	3	5	2

11 (SOLUTIONS)

3	1	6	2	4	5
4	5	2	1	3	6
2	3	4	6	5	1
5	6	1	3	2	4
1	2	5	4	6	3
6	4	3	5	1	2

12 (SOLUTIONS)

2	1	4	3	5	6
6	3	5	1	4	2
4	6	1	2	3	5
3	5	2	6	1	4
1	4	6	5	2	3
5	2	3	4	6	1

6 (SOLUTIONS)

3	5	4	6	2	1
6	2	1	3	4	5
5	3	2	4	1	6
4	1	6	5	3	2
2	4	5	1	6	3
1	6	3	2	5	4

7 (SOLUTIONS)

3	6	5	4	1	2
4	1	2	3	5	6
6	5	1	2	4	3
2	4	3	1	6	5
1	3	6	5	2	4
5	2	4	6	3	1

3 (SOLUTIONS)

2	3	6	5	4	1
4	5	1	2	3	6
3	4	5	6	1	2
6	1	2	4	5	3
5	6	3	1	2	4
1	2	4	3	6	5

4 (SOLUTIONS)

1	2	3	6	4	5
6	5	4	1	3	2
5	1	6	4	2	3
3	4	2	5	1	6
2	6	1	3	5	4
4	3	5	2	6	1

13 (SOLUTIONS)

5	2	6	1	4	3
3	4	1	5	6	2
6	5	4	2	3	1
2	1	3	6	4	5
1	3	5	4	2	6
4	6	2	3	1	5

14 (SOLUTIONS)

1	3	2	5	6	4
4	5	6	1	2	3
3	6	5	2	4	1
2	4	1	3	5	6
5	1	4	6	3	2
6	2	3	4	1	5

8 (SOLUTIONS)

1	3	4	5	6	2
5	6	2	4	1	3
2	1	3	6	4	5
4	5	6	3	2	1
3	4	1	2	5	6
6	2	5	1	3	4

9 (SOLUTIONS)

1	3	4	2	5	6
2	6	5	3	4	1
3	5	1	4	6	2
6	4	2	5	1	3
5	1	3	6	2	4
4	2	6	1	3	5

5 (SOLUTIONS)

1	3	4	5	2	6
2	6	5	1	4	3
3	2	6	4	5	1
4	5	1	3	6	2
6	4	3	2	1	5
5	1	2	6	3	4

15 (SOLUTIONS)

3	2	6	4	1	5
4	5	1	2	6	3
1	6	4	3	5	2
2	3	5	1	4	6
5	1	3	6	2	4
6	4	2	5	3	1

10 (SOLUTIONS)

3	1	4	6	5	2
6	5	2	1	3	4
4	3	6	5	2	1
1	2	5	3	4	6
5	4	1	2	6	3
2	6	3	4	1	5

Solutions

Letter is for #**1** - Earth

Letter is for #**2** - Moon

Letter is for #**3** - Rocket

Letter is for #**4** - Satellite

Letter is for #**5** - UFO

Count the Objects #1 - 9/0/5

Count the Objects #2 - 2/5/4

Count the Objects #3 - 8/6/5

Count the Objects #4 - 4/7/6

Count the Objects #5 - 8/3/1

Count the Objects #6 - 5/6/2

Solutions

PUZZLE-1

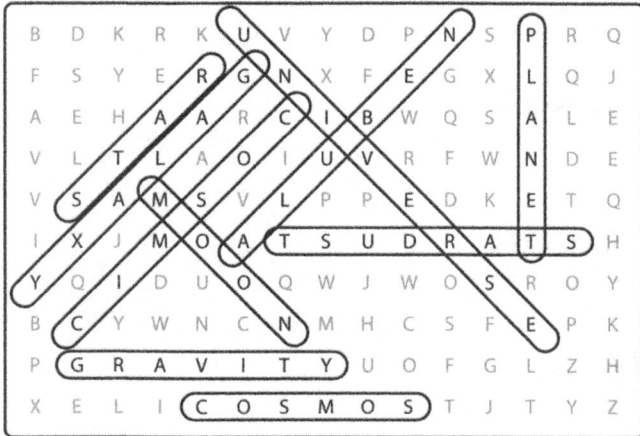

PUZZLE-2

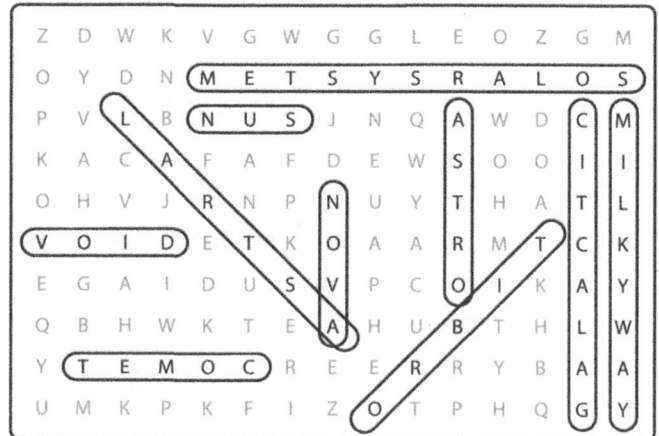

PUZZLE-3

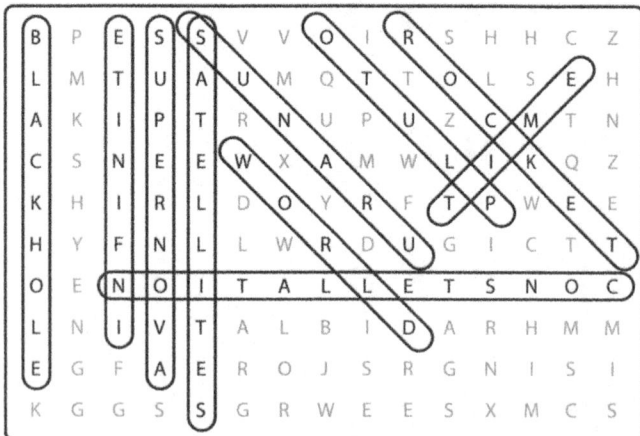

PUZZLE-4

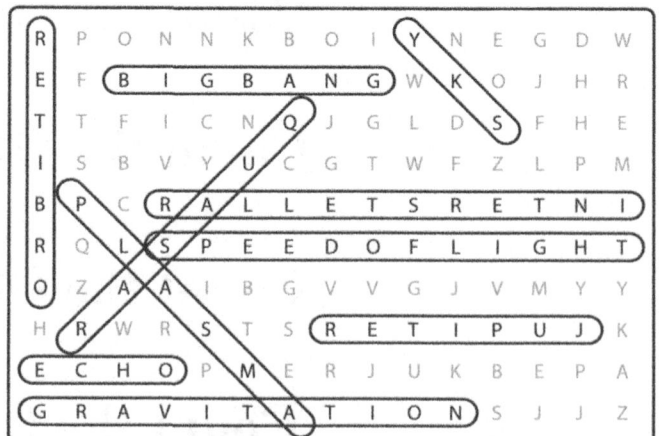

Made in United States
North Haven, CT
29 March 2024